Tokens and Treasures for Life

To Angie –
You are a treasure!
I am so grateful our
paths have crossed –
Love,
Barbara

Tokens and Treasures for Life

Dr. Barbara Baethe Ed.D., L.P.C. & Qunoot Almecci M.S.

ISBN: 0692801758
ISBN 13: 9780692801758
Library of Congress Control Number: 2016919025
Barbara Baethe Dr., Richmond, TEXAS

Table of Contents

Acknowledgments

Qunoot Almecci

First and foremost, all praise belongs to the God who has granted me this amazing opportunity.

To my dear husband, Mir Imdad Ali, thank you for all your love, encouragement, faith and support that you have given me.

To my dear son Arsh Ali, who was three years old at the time of writing this book, thank you for showing me that walls were meant to be written on. I love you so much! May you always embrace the unknown and pursue your passion in life.

To my dearest daughter, Azah Ali, you are such a beautiful inspiration. Without you, this book would not be possible today. I love you so much! May your beautiful smile continue to lighten your journey through life.

To my mom, Atia, and my dad, Syed, thank you for all your encouragement, support and words of wisdom.

To my in-laws, thank you for sharing my happiness and following through with encouragement.

To Dr. Barbara Baethe, thank you for your collaboration and hard work in writing this book

To all those who provided support, encouragement and guidance in making this book possible, thank you.

Dr. Barbara Baethe

I would like to express gratitude and recognition:

To my parents who taught me from my earliest remembrance that all good things come from God and through belief in Him anything is possible.

To my late Grandmother, who thought I was perfect in spite of all of my faults, that I was brilliant before I could write my name and made believe that I could do anything. She would love *Tokens and Treasures for Life.*

To my husband, children and grandchildren for standing by me in all of my endeavors and adventures.

To my dear friend, Mary Nan White, a gifted educator, wife, mother and grandmother extraordinaire and one of the most intelligent individuals I have ever known, for writing the foreword to this book and for always supporting me.

To special friends, Dr. Jane Knapik and Virginia Werlla, who have encouraged me to write a book for the last three decades.

To Qunoot Almecci for sharing her dream of writing a book on success and asking me to share in fulfilling her dream.

To everyone who has touched my life, especially my students over the past four and half decades for giving me the opportunity to share in their educational journey and provided insight into writing this book.

Interior Graphics by
Almaz Tukenov, Student
North American University
Class of 2019

Foreword

It is my pleasure to write this introduction to these vignettes on self-help. The literary work is not an end, but a beginning for the reader. It will provide stepping stones to make dreams and ambitions into reality. From the works of Zig Ziglar, Napoleon Hill, Brian Tracy, Wayne Dyer, and other great leaders on personal success, the student can move his destiny in the direction of his dream.

In Napoleon Hill's introduction to The Law of Success series, he related the story of a young Chicago preacher named Gunsaulus.

> "Gunsaulus published the title of his sermon for the next week in a local newspaper, 'What I Would Do IF I Had a Million Dollars!' Interested in the contents of the sermon, the wealthy packing- house king, Philip D. Armour, decided to attend the church service.
>
> The sermon gave a vision of a school of technology where young students could be given lessons on how to be successful through the ability to think practically, 'learning by doing.' Gunsaulus suggested that the million dollars would be used to set up the learning institution. Armour offered the million dollar startup monies to Gunsaulus. Thus began the Armour Institute of Technology. Armour and Gunsaulus used their imaginations, and Armour's capital to set up a practical 'think tank' to teach success skills." [1]

The readers of this book have been given a glimpse into the imagination of two intelligent and foresighted women who want to share their knowledge and skills concerning how to be successful in life. Both writers realize that they cannot go it alone searching for the process and procedures to make their dreams come true. Each individual decided what she wanted this task to be once completed. Together they planned and sought assistance to meld this literary text into its present form.

To utilize these essays as a catalyst for growth and change, the reader has to be an active participant in the process. The references provide avenues to models, tools, tests, and techniques which can be pathways to follow in studying theory on the streets of success. One key element is that the reader **writes** goals, action plans, thoughts, etc. The reader maintains a journal in which dreams and the goals are scripted. Written notes lead to the accomplishment of dreams. Each topic addressed in this book can be used as a starting point for analysis of thoughts and visions. A quote often used in teaching writing process is: "If you think it, then you ink it, then it will be," alludes to the reader recording thoughts and plans of action. Remember, "The pain of changing the familiar things that you don't like but choose to change is temporary. The pain of not changing the familiar things you don't like, but can change is permanent." I wish each of you success in your venture of self-discovery.

Mary Nan White

Reference:

1. Hill, Napoleon. The Law of Success: The Master Wealth-Builder's Complete and Original Lesson Plan for Achieving Your Dreams, Penguin Publishing Group, 2008. (Originally published as 15 pamphlets, 1925, and then as an eight-book series, 1928.)

Section 1 Tools of Discovery

---

1. The Assessment of Clarity --- Preparation

2. The Foundation of Action --- Purpose

3. The Guarantee of Confidence ---Trust

4. The Credence for Excellence ------------------------------------Potential

CHAPTER 1
The Assessment of Clarity

The Business Dictionary defines values as "important and lasting beliefs or ideals shared by the members of a group." The values are standards concerning what is perceived by the group to be "good or bad and desirable or undesirable" in life. The definition also states that values influence behavior and attitudes to the extent they are used to evaluate a situation. The Business Dictionary defines beliefs as "assumptions and convictions that are held to be true or exist, by an individual or a group, regarding concepts, events, people, and things." [1]

Values are the desires that reveal interaction and relationships. These principles lead and motivate the individual through life. When listing values, most people consider family, health, well-being, happiness, and self-fulfillment. From this perspective, success becomes more than material or financial reward. Happiness is the process of determining personal values and beliefs, so that an individual can pursue a lifestyle that reflects those attributes. Lifestyle is the way of life that is lived by the individual that is guided by values, the principles believed to be of worth. Decision making is controlled by how and why things are valued. [2]

Value systems and belief systems develop early in life. An individual establishes his first values and beliefs based on the systems exhibited by the people, family, that raise him. The values and beliefs that are reflected by caregivers and families are the rudiments of the first value system. Around the pre-adolescent years and throughout high school, peers and society take on the power of influencing, extending, or changing ones values and beliefs. Often these beliefs and the behaviors associated with them are different from those approved by the family value system. The beliefs develop from experiences or evidence that is revealed to the individual. Sports figures, movie stars, and other heroes can influence the immature value and belief systems of a person. Educational institutions, religious training, and the media can also change established values/beliefs. Beliefs may be perceptions or actual thoughts/ events. Beliefs change as the evidence and experiences change. Values are principles or standards of conduct used for justification in decision making. Values are reflected in actions and behavior. Beliefs on the other hand determine how others react to a behavior, situation, or action. [3]

Understanding your values and beliefs is an important step to goal setting. Everything thought, said, or done is based on values. Success is obtained when key values are defined and balanced with desired outcomes. Values are connected to beliefs and motivation level. Evaluating values and beliefs assist an individual in comprehending and changing reactions and feelings. Dawn Barclay in her article about defining core values states "core values are the foundation to authentic living. "Barclay's vision is to help the reader "live in alignment with who he is and to define purpose, why was he put here. Delineating values is a tool that allows one to get in touch with the principles and standards with which he operates." [4]

To become a successful adult who achieves dreams and ambitions, an individual may need to change immature or inappropriate value and belief systems. Value clarification will assist the individual in becoming aware of his personal values and beliefs. The analysis of these systems will demonstrate a comparison to the systems of peers, different groups in society, and successful humans. Critical thinking skills are honed by Socratic questioning to develop an evaluation system for actions and behaviors. As this awareness is revealed, the individual can modify value and belief systems to arrive at more appropriate ones that meet needs of a situation. [5]

Values Clarification assists individuals to identify what values or beliefs lead to a specific situation, action, or behavior. One of the paramount reasons for working with values clarification is to make individuals aware that many diverse but acceptable values can be connected to any situation, action, or behavior. The diverse thinking of a group or society does not have to be the acceptable value or belief of the thinker. Rather, the critical decision making skill of choosing an authentic purpose in life, and following a path to success, can be utilized to prevent feelings of wandering aimlessly without direction or intent. One does not have to follow or accept the beliefs or values of others. The changing of values and beliefs may occur as a result of the process, or the individual may decide to stand steadfast with the original reaction/action and continue to exhibit the values and beliefs of previous situations. Critical decision making skills are developed by the questioning format.

These skills allow the individual to have a conscious awareness of how best to act in any aspect of life.

"The seven criteria for measuring a personal value are:

1. Is your value chosen freely?
2. Is your value chosen from multiple positive alternatives?
3. Is your value chosen after thought and reflection of the pros/cons and consequences?
4. Is your chosen value one you are proud of because you can prize and cherish it?
5. Is your value one that you can publicly affirm?
6. Is your value one that you have acted upon or the display of a belief you have expressed?
7. Is your value part of a pattern that reflects repeated action or consistency?"

The seven criteria will help determine the strength and clarity of values. All seven questions may not be answered for all values, but the more criteria that are reflected for a value the stronger the value system of the individual.

When dealing with values and beliefs, the individual must first know what the outcome of the action, behavior, or situation is to be, so that execution of the steps leads to the desired result. Secondly, the level of motivation necessary to achieve this effect and follow the steps of the path is controlled by the individual's level of awareness. The third factor in choosing the direction of action is to know and understand the personal reason for making the choice and for wanting the outcome. Society is made up of unique individuals. No two people are completely alike. Everything for changing or following value systems and belief systems is found inside each unparalleled human unit from birth. Freedom of choice based on wise, sensible decision making is reflected in rational behavior, called character. [6]

Frank Outlaw, supermarket president of BI-LO, summed up the perspective of why values and beliefs must be critically examined, accepted, or changed to allow the individual to have control of his life. The future of an individual is in expressed words and actions.

"Watch your thoughts, they become words;
Watch your words; they become actions;
Watch your actions, they become habits;

Watch your habits, they become character;
Watch your character, for it becomes your destiny." [7]

References:

1. Business Dictionary.com. http://www.businessdictionary.com/definition/values
2. Marsh, Judith. "Clarifying Personal Values," Distributed by the Clearinghouse at University of Texas. 2007.
3. Akins, Chris. "What is the difference between Values and Beliefs?" 2007. https://www.reference.com/world-view/difference
4. Barclay, Dawn. "Define your Core: The Core Values Workbook and E-mail Series." http://dawnbarclay.com/core-values/
5. Raths, L.E., Harmin, M., and Simon, S.B. Values and Teaching, Second Edition. Columbus, Ohio: Charles E. Merrill, 1978.
6. Jaiper, Jam. "My Life Planning Workbook," 2007. www.achieve-goal-setting-success.com.
7. Outlaw, Frank. (1877, May 18) "What they're Saying," San Antonio Light, Page 28. San Antonio, Texas.

CHAPTER 2
The Foundation of Action

People who succeed have goals, and people who have goals succeed. [1]

No matter how big your ambitions are, the only way to get there is to prepare a plan that is built around your goals. Have you ever written New Year's Resolutions with the best intentions, but did not achieve them because of a case of "set-and-forget?"

Goal setting is not a product, but a process. The procedures permit an individual to achieve his heart's desires through the use of a GPS system. The system is a plan of action that if followed gives direction to the individual in the journey down life's pathways.

Zig Ziglar at his Ziglar Training System determined "that only 3% of the people in the USA set goals, and they are among the wealthiest people in the nation." [2]

The first lesson he suggests is to DREAM! Write down at least 25 things you want to be, to do, or to have.

Remember that Disney says,

> "A dream is a wish your heart makes
> When you're fast asleep.
> In dreams you lose your heartaches.
> Whatever you wish for, you keep.
> Have faith in your dreams and someday
> Your rainbow will come smiling through
> No matter how your heart is grieving
> If you keep on believing
> The dream that you wish will come true." [3]

The second step after you record your dreams is to wait 24 to 48 hours and look at the list. Analyze each dream and answer the question–Why? You should be able to state a one sentence reason you want to be, do, or have this dream. If you can't make the statement, cross it off your list because it is not something you value, and it should not become a goal.

The third procedure is to ask yourself the following questions about every dream on the list:

- "Is it really MY goal?
- Is it morally right and fair to everyone concerned?
- Is it consistent with my other goals?
- Can I emotionally commit myself to finish this goal?
- Can I 'see' myself reaching this goal?"

Cross off the dream (goal) if any goal is given a "no" for any of these five questions.

Process step number four is to ask yourself the following seven questions about each dream that remains on the list, and if you cannot answer "yes" to at least one of the seven questions, cross that dream (goal) off your list.

"Will reaching this goal (dream). . .

1. Make me happier?
2. Make me healthier?
3. Make me more prosperous?
4. Win me more friends?
5. Give me peace of mind?
6. Make me more secure?
7. Improve my relationships with others? "

Procedure five is to divide the dreams (goals) that are left into three categories:

1. Short-range goals (one month or less to achieve this goal),
2. Intermediate goals (one month to one year to achieve this goal), and
3. Long-range goals (one year or more to achieve this goal).

Most of the goals you set should be definite and specific. Be sure that you do not try to undertake too many goals at one time. Four goals in each section is the maximum that you should attempt, and even this may be too many. Remember that short-range goals allow you to keep focused and make achievements toward your other two categories of goals. Long-range goals allow you to grow and change to reach your potential. Intermediate goals may lead to bigger goals. The plans of action will keep you on track and moving toward success.

In summary, Zig Ziglar has listed seven steps to make sure you are setting goals that can be achieved:

"1. **Identify your goals**. Your goals arise from your Dream List. You must identify what you value in life and what is important to you. This is a very personal look at your belief system. You cannot rely on someone else to evaluate and analyze your experiences, your priorities, or beliefs. Is this a goal you want or is it one that someone else wants you to achieve?

2. **Identify people and organizations that can help you meet your goals.** You must identify the support network that will assist you in meeting your goals. Be positive in your search for these groups and individuals. Be sure that they will be honest with you, and inspire you to meet your objectives.

3. **Set a deadline for meeting your goals.** Goals need to have a time when they will be achieved. If you do not set a time line for achieving each goal, you will never know if you have completed the task. Breaking the goals into the three categories will assist you in establishing realistic timelines for completion.

4. **Define any obstacles to accomplish your goals.** Be sure you know the requirements that are needed to meet your goals. Roadblocks are present in most projects; the decision to strive to overcome the blockage is if the process will get you further on your journey toward your destination. Focus on the big picture, so you do not become distracted by the barriers on the pathway.

5. **Identify the skills and knowledge needed to meet your goals.** If your goal is too large, divide the goal into smaller goals which can be accomplished in a manner that leads toward the completion of the bigger ones.

6. **Develop a <u>plan of action</u> for reaching your goals.**
   WRITE:
   a. Your goals,
   b. The list of people and organizations that can help you meet your goals (Be sure that you know how and why these support groups and individuals can and will encourage you),
   c. The benchmarks for the accomplishment of sub-goals,
   d. A definite, specific deadline for the completion of the goal,
   e. Any obstacles that you foresee getting into your pathway (Explain how you will overcome these barriers.),
   f. The skills and knowledge needed, and
   g. How you will obtain these skills and the knowledge.
   This written document will be your **action plan**.
7. **List benefits of reaching your goals.** Now write the benefit to you of achieving these goals. This should be personal; it is part of "why" you have written goals." [4]

Brian Tracy in his workbook, <u>Strategic Setting for Success Guide</u>, identifies two factors that result in personal success: the person knows specifically what he wants, and is determined to achieve the goal no matter the price. [5] "Begin now! Do something every day to achieve your goals and never give up."

References:

1. Jaiper, Jam. "My Life Planning Workbook," 2007. www.achieve-goal-setting-success.com.
2. Ziglar, Zig. "Zig Ziglar on Goal Setting," <u>Goals 2 Go.</u> (2002-2011). No Dream Too Big.LLC, http://goals2go.com/articles/zig-ziglar-goal-setting.htm.
3. David, Mack, A. Hoffman, and Jerry Livingston. "A Dream is a Wish Your Heart Makes." *Cinderella*, Disney Productions. 1950.
4. Ziglar, Zig. "How to Be a Winner." (2002). CD A Nightingale-Conant Production, Simon and Schuster Audio.
5. Tracy, Brian. <u>Strategic Goal Setting for Success.</u> (2013). Solana Beach, CA: Brian Tracy International, www.briantracy.com.

CHAPTER 3
The Guarantee of Confidence

Many people find it difficult to trust others. I believe that to trust others, I must begin by trusting myself. I must learn to trust my instincts, my decisions, and my choices. In this day and age with all the noise and chaos, it gets harder to listen to my inner self and I easily become a victim of self-doubt and fear. I am a student of this massive classroom, the world; my education extends far beyond the brick and mortar classrooms, to the midst of society's lessons where I have obtained endless knowledge and skills. I am in a world where technology and communications are everywhere. The news media and telecasts connect me with the farthest reaches of this planet and space. Every crack or fissure that appears in the cosmos is accentuated for the negative and sometimes the positive. Who should I trust to tell the truth and the facts?

I can remember at least at one point in time my trust has been compromised by a friend, a loved one, a colleague, or an employer. How did that make me feel? Did I ever make a choice to confront the other party who violated my trust? What about a commitment I made to myself, what happened when I did not maintain my own trust? Who did I blame? Which is a greater disappointment the violation of trust from another or me? I think my greatest disappointment is the inability to trust myself. During my time of meditation, I mulled in my mind what happened that caused me to distrust myself. I questioned that my decision was not mine alone, but controlled by someone else's comments or actions. Since I am a thinking person, I tried to justify all the reasons for not completing a task, or failing to follow through on a decision. The distrust made me feel hollow. In my feeling of inadequacy, I reached out for support for my decision to help spread the blame to others. I felt that I had betrayed myself which reiterates my thoughts that the concept of trust is a sensitive one.

I can never truly know for sure if someone will sabotage my trust. I have no control over others, but I do have control over myself. The person that I really need to build a trusting relationship with is I. That means never giving up on my dreams or ambitions. No other person can hurt me or offend me, unless I give them that power. I am in control of my life. My reactions and choices determine how I feel about situations. I must trust myself to believe that I am capable of accomplishing my goals. I must believe that I have what it takes to begin a task and see it through to completion. Most of all I must have the ability to follow through to create my desired results so I strengthen my belief in my own worth.

Although there are many principles I have outlined my favorite top three when it comes to defining trust:

1. Trust yourself: Develop self-trust and belief in your own skills, talents and abilities. You have within you the secrets of the universe coiled in your DNA. Your body is working around the clock to provide you the greatest support, if you could just trust it enough. Be open minded enough to hear the views, thoughts and opinions of others. Peruse the teachings of various factions to extract what is necessary and valuable for you. Listen to yourself because no one knows you better than yourself. Take the time out of your hectic life and have a conversation with your inner self. Spend time in quiet meditation on a daily basis. Give yourself accolades for what you have accomplished. Analyze the bits and pieces of your day to pat yourself on the back for moving forward toward your goals and priorities. Write down any changes you will make in the days ahead to move consistently and constantly toward your priorities. "If we did all the things we were capable of doing, we would literally astound ourselves." Thomas Edison [1]

2. Trust the Universe: You are exactly how you were meant to be. You are on a path of great success. You were placed as a critical component to help with the creation and development of this universe. No matter what your shortcomings, your flaws, or what you think it is that you lack, you were created as planned. You have something greater to offer to this universal classroom. No one or thing was created without purpose. It is your job to determine your purpose in life and how best to accomplish that purpose. Remember that you only have one chance at life. You must use every minute of every day to demonstrate your values and beliefs.

3. Trust your failures: Often times we perceive our failures or challenges as a loss. We must learn from our mistakes. These trials or tests, often called screw-ups and failures can serve a constructive purpose. You must trust that amid even the greatest loss and challenge, there is a lesson to be learned. You may not see it at the time, but trust that it is necessary for you to have this experience so you may excel and meet your potential. Everything is charged with duty in accordance with its ability. Thomas Edison was described at an early age by his teachers as "too stupid to learn anything." He was fired from his first two jobs and described as "non-productive." When Edison was inventing the incandescent light bulb, he made 1,000 unsuccessful attempts. A newspaper reporter questioned his feelings about failing 1,000 times. Edison replied, "I didn't fail 1,000 times. The light bulb was an invention with 1,000 steps." [2]

My experiences and challenges have made me who I am today. One of my greatest obstacles that I have overcome in the more recent years has been my ability to trust that what I have to say is worth it. Being surrounded with everyone's opinions and thoughts via web opinions or social gatherings, I have mustered up the courage to speak what I feel needs to be said. This book has been a long time coming and I have written it in many ways. I never trusted my words or thoughts enough to write them out. I'm sure it has to do with flashbacks of my trust being violated at some point in time. At some point in life I had to let go of those fears that have held me back. I need to redirect that energy to fulfill my passions which I deeply desired to do so many years ago. So if you find yourself with your trust being compromised, pick up the pieces and believe in yourself once again knowing that this time around it is different because you are in control.

References:

1. A 4th Course of Chicken Soup for the Soul. (1997). Canfield, Jack, Mark Victor Hansen, Hanoch McCarty, and Meladee McCarty. eds. Health Communications, Inc. Deerfield Beach, Florida, p. 263.
   Additional resource is: My Reference Frame. https://www.myreferenceframe.com/
2. University of Kentucky, "But They Did Not Give Up." Thomas Edison, Inventor. http://www.uky.edu/~eushe2/Pajares/OnFailingG.html

CHAPTER 4
The Credence for Excellence

Values and beliefs are developed throughout life. Values are the basis for behavior and motivation. In abstract form, values provide a description of self-worth, personal meaning, and desire for achievement. These statements of purpose are deemed important enough to take specific steps to achieve, thus goals and actions demonstrate the level of value. From the goals and actions grow behaviors and motivation. [1] Values that most often are listed are: "success, loyalty, truthfulness, charity, service, family, friendship, respect, and integrity." "Beliefs contain judgments and the action to achieve this belief in the world. Beliefs are maps that shape reality. Beliefs are related to values since they provide the experiences which are the context by which behaviors are judged." [2]

What do you believe? My answer to this is found in a song made famous by Elvis Presley called, "I Believe."

I Believe

I believe for every drop of rain that falls
A flower grows.
I believe that somewhere in the darkest night
A candle glows.
I believe for everyone that goes astray
Someone will come to show the way.
I believe, I believe. [3]

I believe in myself as I am. I believe I have a purpose in life in spite of my flaws, shortcomings and inabilities, I know that all of these components make me who I am.

I know that my abilities outnumber my inabilities. I am stronger than the weakest part of me. I am focused and driven in my ambitions towards executing my lifelong goals.

I may not be perfect, but I do have stories to tell and experiences to share. I have my own viewpoints which are valid. I need to prove myself and compete with myself so I meet the standards that I have set. I do not need to worry about what others think of me or compete with others for success. I hold myself accountable for my accomplishments and successes. I am responsible for my failures and defeats. Taking responsibility for my achievements and my screw-ups is necessary for me to believe in myself. I believe in my mission and purpose in life. I know that the only person I can change is me.

I believe in today. I was blessed with another day of life and health I realize that the only time I have control over is the here and now. "Yesterday is history, tomorrow is a mystery, today is a gift, that is why it is called the present." [4]

I believe in my ability to appreciate and achieve my goals in the universe. I believe in the 24 hours of today, I can take little steps to accomplish big goals. Many people spend their time worrying about something in the past they cannot change, or something in the future that may happen. Both are a futile waste of time and energy.

Lastly, I believe in **You**! I make it a point to find the good in people and believe in their abilities. I believe in the individuals who have yet to cross my path. Whether you are my spouse, my partner, my child, my colleague, my peer or a student, I believe in you because you carry a piece within you that contributes to my life. I encourage you to adopt positive affirmations that reflect what you believe and value. You must *believe* in yourself and others. To become paranoid or fear personal abilities will create a negative aura that will further destroy your self-worth and cause you to go astray. I believe that we are all equally important in the scheme of things on this earth. Positive thoughts lead to positive words which lead to positive actions. Habits can be corrected. It takes approximately 21 days to correct a bad habit. I remember moving my kitchen trash to my laundry room to avoid little hands from turning it over. It took me at least 21 days to get in the habit of stepping into the new location to deposit my garbage. Don't give up on yourself.

Realize that we all have a gift, a potential. Some are artists, singers, writers, students, motivational speakers, doctors, teachers, plumbers, carpenters, janitors, and lawyers. The most unfortunate among us are those that do see their potential. They choose to hide or not use their talents and skills. Some tend to misuse their knowledge and skills. I feel it is everyone's responsibility to contribute to make the world a better place and ultimately utilize our personal talents. The power of believing in your abilities and yourself will shine new light into your life. You may seek that support from an external source, but beware that the responses you receive may be negative stimuli in the form of rejection and taunting. I challenge you to be your own cheerleader first. You know yourself best. Then secondly, remember that I believe in you. You are a worthy, talented individual. You have potential to become a positive influence in society. It is my desire that you find inspiration to pursue whatever is your passion. Through self-esteem you can find peace in your heart and the courage to break down barriers. Your words, thoughts, opinions do matter. This universe is missing what you are holding back. Open your mind and give of your talents. Seek to find your purpose in life.

Many times I have wished to return to my old self of a ten year old child to change my fears and negativity. I cannot go back so I must begin today to submit written articles. The change has occurred because I have received encouragement from others and now believe in my self-worth. To find yourself when you don't know where you belong, start with self. You are good enough. Your work may not be perfect, but it will improve with practice. The world is made up of humans with flaws that are making changes for the betterment of the world. If you see an individual err, learn from that person's mistakes. You do not have to jump off a mountain to know if the ground at the bottom is hard. To become what you want and do what you love, you must tackle your demons within. I don't need everyone to like my work and understand me. I am doing this because I enjoy it and it makes me feel alive. This is what belief in self feels like. It is pure bliss and contentment to be writing a guide to help others. I hope that you experience this happiness that I am feeling. Remember

"You Can Do It!"

I wake up every morning telling myself these three statements.

I believe in myself.
I believe in today.
I believe in you.

References:

1. Atkins, Chris. (2010, August 11). "The Nature of Values." <u>Skills for Successful Living.</u>

2. Atkins, Chris.(2010, August 18). "The Difference between Beliefs and Values." <u>Skills for Successful Living.</u>

3. Whittaker, Roger. "I Believe", (1957).
Sung by Elvis Presley. Retrieved September 5, 2016. 2:00 PM.
https://www.youtube.com/watch?v= ODtExxkWOws

4. Dickinson, Emily. Poem #1292, "Yesterday is History." Reworded by Bill Keane.

CHAPTER 5
The Sequence for Performance

"Set priorities for your goals. A major part of successful living lies in the ability to put first things first. Indeed, the reason most major goals are not achieved is that we spend our time doing second things first." [1]

Stephen Covey in his book, <u>The Seven Habits of Highly Effective People</u>, states that to create a life congruent with answers, to complete goals, and to change habits; an individual must breakdown, analyze, sequence, and follow a specific plan. Priority decision making means to *put first things first*. The process of sequencing and evaluating concepts to manage the order of completion is accomplished through self-discipline. Deciding what is to be a top priority means establishing a purpose, setting a clear sense of direction, and determining the personal value for successful completion of the task. [2]

Albert E.N. Gray in his essay, "The Common Denominator of Success," determined that setting priorities was the factor that was shared by all successful people. Gray analyzed hard work, good luck, a repertoire of good habits, assistance from intelligent people, and good grades. All were necessary attributes for success which defined the process, but it was motivation that drove the procedure. Simplified, Gray stated that "The common denominator of success - - - the secret of success of every man who has ever been successful - - - lies in the fact that he formed the habit of doing things that failures don't like to do." Gray determined that sequencing the order of performing activities had to be based on more cognitive thought than natural likes and dislikes or even natural preferences and prejudices. The order of priorities of a successful man looked at the success of the end result, not at the success or pleasure of the method of obtaining the result. Along with listing and performing tasks based on the desired end result, the next factor was the establishment of consciously forming good habits.

The list of priorities had to be based on a practical purpose, not necessarily logical or visionary. Needs are based on logic, but wants are based on sentiment and emotion. Wants and desires motivate the individual to be, to do, and to create. "The strength of the purpose of the goal is stronger than the dislike of the task." [3]

Time management evolves around an individual organizing and completing priorities that can lead to more self-control. From a clarification of values, comparison of the worth of tasks based on those values, the establishment of goals that reflect those values, the next step in setting priorities is determining the daily planning and order of executing the activities that mirror these values and lead us toward our ultimate destination. Priorities usually fall into two categories: urgent and Important. Urgent matters are visible. They must be attended. They may be pleasant, but may also be unimportant. Important has to do with results which are related to values, missions in life, and high priority goals.

Some tasks fall in both categories and must be dealt with immediately due to being "crises" or "problems." If the activity is urgent but not important, it probably is a list of priorities and expectations of someone other than the author. Not either urgent or important are activities that probably could be handled by someone else and are not a priority of the individual. The most valuable priorities for obtaining results and reaching success at goals are those which are not urgent, but are important. These priorities are described as tasks which prevent trouble, build relationships, recognize new opportunities, develop a personal mission statement, perform long-range planning, provide preventative maintenance, prepare for future performance, and even participate in healthy living and exercise. This category holds all the priorities that if performed on a regular basis "would make a tremendous positive difference in the individual's life."

"The hardest thing in life is to learn which bridges to cross and which bridges to burn." [4] Setting priorities is often the process of comparing needs versus wants. This process makes the activity more emotional and sentimental than intellectual. Making decisions about such matters as prioritizing activities for dieting and exercising to lose weight or budgeting to save money require the individual to exert self-discipline, commitment, and a focus on the purposeful result obtained by the task. Procrastination sets in and the priority scale tips to either a lower value or no allotment of time on the schedule. Major emphasis must be given to the important priorities whose achievement will improve life, and aid in obtaining a successful completion of dreams and ambitions. The higher order priorities reflect a simple, clear explanation of what is being done, why it is being done, and how it relates to other priorities and goals. [5]

Successful team leaders have strong priorities awareness which is powerful. They have determined what is most important and are able to share the reasons with the team. The hierarchy of priorities can be used to redirect secondary issues and distractions back to the problem or project. The focus is always successful completion of top goals.

Along with setting priorities, the successful person develops the ability to say "no." A person's priority list can be destroyed by his inability to decline to take on tasks that are not conducive to meeting his personal mission and purpose in life. A priority list that is constantly changing is not a list of personal priorities that are urgent or important to the individual; rather the list is controlled by outside forces that prevent successful completion of projects. A person who cannot say "no" to outside forces is doomed to failure.

Priorities point to activities that are important to the individual's health, family, career, financial future, or entertainment. Non-essential activities are replaced with tasks and projects that move the person closer to completion of goals. Long-term projects are divided into manageable units that can be completed early and build toward the ultimate result. Work on priorities can be scheduled at optimum times in the work day or week so more can be done in less time. Tasks that are similar in nature can be scheduled together; it is easier to respond to all e-mails, phone calls, or texts at the same time rather than as they become apparent during the day. Tasks can be delegated or eliminated from a priority list if they are not high on the hierarchy. [6]

References:

1. McKain, Robert. "Set Priorities for your goals." (Quotation #9491). Poor Man's College. Aapex Software. Promotional CD.
2. Covey, Stephen R. (1989). The Seven Habits of Highly Effective People. New York: Simon and Schuster.
3. Gray, Albert E. N. (1940). "The Common Denominator of Success," Speech given to National Association of Life Underwriters, Philadelphia, Pennsylvania,
4. Russell, David. Scottish guitarist. Thinkexist.com/quotes/david-russell

5. Trapani, Gina. "How Priorities Make Things Happen." Rev. of <u>Making Things Happen: Mastering Project Management</u>, by Scott Berkun. (9 July 2008). http://lifehacker.com/398119/how-priorities-make-things-happen

6. Novakowski, Andrea. "What are your Priorities for Your Business?" <u>The Online Self Improvement Encyclopedia: Self-Growth.com</u>. (30 December 2011). http://www.selfgrowth.com/print/3803711

CHAPTER 6
The Ascertainment of Self-Worth

Since the times of the Greeks, knowledge of self-understanding has been dissected and assimilated. The phrases "Know thyself," and "The unexamined life is not worth living." are quotes that have been around for centuries. The discovery of the vast array of qualities and characteristics of the self contribute mystery and intrigue for one toiling through the daily grind. The opportunities that lay before you are minute compared to the potential that lies within you. Ralph Waldo Emerson so aptly stated, "What lies behind us and what lies before us are tiny matters compared to what lies within us." [1]

The individual can choose to wander through life from pillar to post unable to successfully complete most journeys. This individual is unhappy and feels like life is without purpose. Or, the individual can choose to identify his potential and move toward completing his reason for being in the universe. The latter being identifies his passion and feels worthy of his accomplishments.

Other people may make suggestions and provide support for the individual along the path of self-discovery, but the choices are personal. The only changes that will make sense are the changes that make sense to the individual. People who pressure or push to mold an individual ignore the fact that self-worth and self-respect are developed when the individual analyzes his own belief and value systems. Each individual longs for self-realization, and to be in control of his future. The future is only limited by the limits an individual places on himself. Life does not require perfection; life's pursuits are only limited by one's vision.

Change occurs when the individual acquires self-realization, and then sets in motion a plan of action and growth. Self-understanding can be rewarding. Self-awareness allows one to get more out of life, and not be an obstacle in his search for progress.

The struggle of examining self-worth, setting limits based on self-respect, and building self-esteem contribute to a feeling of wholeness.

People who wanted to be popular and well liked often forfeit self-respect for the act of "fitting in." As Polonius so appropriately stated in <u>Hamlet</u>, Act 1 Scene 3,

"To thine own self be true,
And it must follow, as the night the day,
Thou canst not then be false to any man." [2]

When an individual journeys down uncharted paths in life, he must always apply self-honest and self-respect to decisions; so that these choices will lead to growth. Thus, the individual will blossom. One who studies self-sabotage can prevent a reoccurrence of actions and behaviors that destroy productivity and motivation. Another gain obtained from self-realization is an awareness of the motivation of others. The individual who has self-awareness and self-understanding can discern the feelings and motivations behind the behaviors of others.

In the journey of self-discovery, the individual will examine his emotions and the motivation behind certain behaviors and actions. An individual tends to set limits that hinder achievement, love, joy, progress, and accomplishments. One must embrace the challenges that life throws out. These difficulties build a stronger inner self that develops critical components of the unique whole that can confront future pitfalls.

Adapting this perspective in life changes the individual into a conquering hero who sees future challenges as routes to deeper meaning for the inner self. Every experience, every moment is a learning point, an opportunity for growth.

The next section is an activity that can lead to self-discovery. Divide a piece of paper, 8 ½ by 10 inches, into four equal parts with a set of perpendicular lines. In the top left quadrant, write an experience or time that was difficult or challenging in life. Maybe this was a time when a course grade was below expectations, or a doctor's diagnosis shattered dreams. In the quadrant on the right top, describe initial reaction to the experience, list and describe feelings, behaviors, emotions, etc. In the bottom left quadrant, describe and list feelings, behaviors, emotions, etc. that were experienced when the situation was rectified or time had allowed acceptance of the issue. In the bottom right quadrant, list strengths and details about the inner self that grew from struggling with the challenge. This last quadrant tends to be longer and more specific because every situation can provide positive reinforcements to self and growth.

Low self-esteem generates "happiness anxiety." When an individual values himself, and can cope with challenges in life, one believes in his right to be happy. One with low self-esteem tends to feel unworthy of happiness or deserving of a good life. Depression and self-destruction often are the course of one who feels his life is doomed to "bad" luck. Fear of the unknown often lead to patterns of behavior that annihilate an individual through self-sabotage. Anxiety builds and the solution to clearing the cause of the anxiousness is to destroy the thing that would make one happy. This may be through hurtful words, violent acts, or deserting in a relationship. The individual shields himself from new relationships, new pathways, and new ideas because he knows where the old destructive ways lead him. The old behavior is known and familiar thus unhappiness appears to be comfortable.

To overcome fear of the unknown, the individual must confront and define the fears. Fear no longer has power when it is faced as an adversary. The subconscious mind is forced to analyze the composition of the fear and how to change the reaction to destroy the fear. One finds personal fulfillment and happiness through autonomy and reaching beyond self-imposed limits on our dreams. The individual discovers the "real me" and puts away desires to please others, parents, peers, etc. The only person who has to be pleased is himself.

The first step to obtaining self-discovery is to accept one's self and silence the inner "critic." [3] The individual defines self-concept, self-esteem, and self-confidence. Along with an analysis of self, the person must identify attitudes, beliefs, and values. From this study, the individual notes the level of positivity of attributes like creativity, imagination, curiosity and motivational enthusiasm, which can aid him in building resilience, flexibility, and resourcefulness. Through self-awareness, the person looks at thinking patterns and how these routines assisted or harmed him. One must become a lifelong learner who is willing to adapt to meet certain goals. To maintain stamina and strength, the person must seek daily exercise, eat a balanced diet, maintain routine sleep patterns, and strive for day-to-day healthy living. Self-discovery confirms the theory that each person possesses all the attributes necessary to be successful in life. Every individual is born with the qualities and aptitudes necessary to complete a purposeful life. An individual who examines his unique self for idiosyncrasies and opportunities becomes more whole. The wholeness allows greater self-happiness and the ability to help others.

Dr. Harry Emerson Fosdick is quoted as saying that "What seems to matter most is how you see yourself." Fosdick felt that each individual had the power to imagine success or failure. Dr. Fosdick stated that "Great living starts with a picture, held in your imagination, of what you would like to do or be." [4]

References:

1. Branden, Nathaniel. "The Art of Self-discovery," Honoring the Self and How to Raise your Self-esteem.
2. Shakespeare, William. Hamlet, Act 1, Scene 3.
3. "Self-Discovery for You." 2016. http://www.self-discovery-for-you.com/
4. Maltz, Maxwell. "Self-Image," (22 January 2013). Grief and Mourning.Com. http://griefandmourning.com/self-image.

Section 2 Inquiry of Balance

7. The Structure of Procedures--Organization

8. The Act of Motivation ---Inspiration

9. The Attributes of Control ---Patience

10. The Publication of Intent--- Communication

11. The Manifestation of Honesty --Integrity

12. The Perception of the Moment --Opportunity

CHAPTER 7
The Structure of Procedures

Organization includes but is not limited to having an orderly arrangement for performing daily tasks in the global picture of completing an activity. Thus, organization is having a uniform method of locating and retrieving materials and references. It also is present in the development of goals, priorities, values, and beliefs. One other unit of organization that you can control is time.

Time Management involves organizing your day to accomplish the things you need to get done. Baltasar Gracian stated that, "All that really belongs to us is time; even he who has nothing else has that." [1] Everybody has the same amount of time in a week: 168 hours. You are responsible for your use of your time. You can control your time by making lists of priorities and activities that are necessary to complete tasks. You must communicate your values and beliefs clearly so that others know why your time is scheduled.

Some tips for time management are: [2]

1. You set goals and priorities to determine your sense of direction. Make your daily planner indicate the time and task you are going to require of yourself. If you have a long and difficult assignment or task facing you, your first response should be to study the entire problem and plan the approach, develop an action plan, and follow the steps to complete the assignment or task. Planning takes time but saves time in the end. Write down your goals for the task/assignment. Be sure that your plan includes priorities in the time schedule. The sooner you put your "teeth into a job," the sooner you will determine what you will need to do to complete the task/assignment. Once you develop a schedule, stick to it. [3] [4]

2. Refer to your analysis of core beliefs and values to strengthen your GPS to direct you to complete tasks that are necessary to accomplish your goals. Once you determine your schedule, write it down. A good day's work should be measured by how many of the bits and pieces that complete the task/assignment you have completed so that you are ready to handle big tasks the next study or writing session. References and research come before the finished product; you should not write your outline after writing your paper. Research and points of reference are gathered before writing the rough draft of an essay. Stress the results, not the activity. Put first things first. [5] [6]

3. You must break large jobs into smaller increments. For example, studying for a Friday test does not mean waiting until Thursday night to read the assigned chapters, study the class notes, and write possible test questions with answers. Instead, you should start early. Divide the chapters so that you cover at least one chapter per night. Notes and possible questions with answers can be written for each chapter on that night. By Wednesday night you should have covered all chapters, now review class notes and write questions /answers on the notes. Thursday night is a review of all chapter and class notes. Included in the Thursday review should be asking and answering the possible questions you have developed. [7] [8]

4. Quality control of your time may mean listening to your biological clock to determine the best time in a 24 hour span to do work. You should attack your most difficult tasks during your peak performance time. Do not waste time. "Time is the only thing in life that once it is gone can never be resurrected." [9] Even five minutes standing in a line may be the time needed to review those note cards, study memory work, or read and review for a test. Know the number of major tasks that you can work on at one time. Be sure to not over commit. Remember you set priorities. Always be sure that your goal is being met. If you attempt less in a time frame, you prevent mistakes and feel satisfaction at completing a task with finesse. Perfection is necessary if you are a brain surgeon or airline pilot, but not required to create a quality English essay. Remember that you need to discriminate and judge the steps to complete tasks or resolve situations so that if perfection is not necessary, quality will be utilized. [10] [11]

5. Don't fall into the Procrastination Trap. A common trap that many people fall into when it comes to meeting their goals is procrastination. Procrastination is defined by Webster as, "the act of putting off doing something until a future time." [12] Procrastination can keep you from meeting self-imposed deadlines and self-set goals. Procrastination can also be positive if you put off doing things that are not important or necessary for you to meet your goals and priorities. [13]

6. Your schedule must have balance with a time for sleeping, eating, leisure, exercising, and working. Every so often, you may need to take a break from important work. This is acceptable since working straight through on a project without stepping back and checking your direction and points of reference can make you stale and tired. Take time to evaluate and check your direction. Save time by doing it right the first time, and you will not have to do it over. [14] [15]

7. Are there any activities that you want to complete as soon as you get more time? Do these activities relate to accomplishing your goals and priorities? If yes, then make time for them now. You must use rational decision making by getting facts, setting goals, investigating alternatives, and determining negative consequences before making decisions about your project. Implementation of the schedule should be the last stage of the task or assignment. Evaluate the cost of getting what you want at the end of the journey. Be sure you can afford the sacrifice that must be made for success at the task, then invest in a high quality use of time. Remember to be ruthless with time, but gracious with people. Relationships need to be fostered and included on your time schedule. [16] [17]

8. You must address interruptions as to the value they have in completing the present tasks and in completing future tasks and priorities. Be sure the value of the interruption is not a fear of failure or a fear of rejection of a relationship. As Franklin Delano Roosevelt so appropriately stated, ". . . the only thing we have to fear is fear itself." [18] Research has shown that you do not work better under pressure, rather, you work faster. Your best work is when you have a method, schedule, and purpose for performing a task. [19] [20]

References:

1. Meier, J. D. Time Management Quotes. Accessed (20 August 2016). 7:00 AM. (Quote from Balthasar Gracian, a Jesuit priest in the 1600"s, "The Art of Worldly Wisdom.") http:// sourcesofinsight.com/time-management-quotes

2. Pain, Sue. "Time Management Exercise." You Tube. Retrieved 20 August 2016. 8:00 AM. https://www.youtube.com/watch?v=UyM3idwXi-o

3. Grant, Patricia. Reading and Study Skills, "Effective Time Management". New York: Prentice Hall, 1989.

4. "11 Top Tips for Effective Time Management," Josie Chun. www.careerfaqs.com.au/news/news-and-views/11–top-tips-for-effective-time-management

5. Grant, op.cit.

6. Chun, op.cit.

7. Grant, op.cit.

8. Chun, op.cit.

9. Grant, op.cit.

10. Ibid, Grant,

11. Chun, op.cit.

12. The American Heritage Dictionary of the English Language, William Morris, ed. Dallas: Houghton Mifflin Company, 1975.

13. Tasso. "Want to Beat Procrastination? Watch out for these 5 traps!" YouTubeRolemodelU.com Video 11:49 Script available on http://rolemodelu.com/blog.beat-procrastination Retrieved 20 August 2016. 8:30 AM.

14. Grant, op.cit.

15. Chun, op.cit.

16. Grant, op.cit.

17. Chun, op.cit.

18. Roosevelt, Franklin D. "Inaugural Address, March 4, 1933, Published by Samuel Rosenman, ed., The Public Papers of Franklin D. Roosevelt, Volume Two: The Year of Crisis, 1933. (New York: Random House, 1938) pp. 11-16.

19. Grant, op.cit.

20. Chun, op.cit.

CHAPTER 8
The Act of Motivation

"Positive thinking won't let you do anything, but positive thinking will let you do everything better than negative thinking will." [1]

Zig Ziglar revealed the following statistics from daily life: 90% of the input in our minds is of a negative nature. He stated that the average 18 year old has been told 148,000 times "No" or "You can't do it." This guru of motivation and inspiration felt that decisions and ambitions must be structured with heartfelt enthusiasm so the individual can commit to change. Because the seeker is committed to change, he will search and undertake training to make the changes necessary to accomplish the decisions and ambitions. Training brings about behavioral changes, but most of all good training develops a "winning attitude." [2]

My inspiration to write this book grew from the many books and articles I have read. I grew up in a home where there was a basement full of old dusty books and dated clothing articles. My mom used to save clothing items to recycle into a new abstract design or sofa wear. My father saved and read books which included everything from the "Children's Highlights" to books on complex research findings on modern genetics. On days that I wanted to be a mystery detective, I trekked to this dingy scary basement which was filled with unknown critters amongst the arrays of magic and intrigue. I would find a seat on a huge black trash bag full of old expensive clothes hoping to come across a stimulating enigma, at the same time trying to avoid any spider that I had disturbed from his contented self-made environment. These were my finest memories of childhood which inspired me to write my book. I had dreamed of writing and these diverse and wonderful literature selections encouraged me to strike out for my dream. My father has always said, "You will never find all of what you're looking for in one place, it's up to you to extract the source of information that is relevant to you." His encouragement allowed me to extract the experiences that applied to my commitment to reach my ambition. Like artists, scientists and researchers before me, I had to study to create my new designs and images.

The first step to finding a "source of inspiration" is look at you. Everyone's inspiration is different. Analyze your goals, beliefs, values, dreams, and attitude to find the motivation to move down the path toward success. Some people have materialistic motives such as money, cars, houses, or clothes. Others need to satisfy emotional desires for love, or to find revenge. Your beliefs and values should be reflected in the actions and behaviors you utilize to find your place in the universe. If your motivation is of a negative nature, your attitude will be reflected in your behavior. I encourage you to seek out positive aspirations that will take you to new heights and lead you to a life where you have no regrets. Remember that pitfalls and crevasses on the climb to your dream are only small pauses to reflect on the steps you have been taking. These detours can be a source of inspiration. Be sure that you are moving in the right direction. Allow yourself the time to reflect on your training and events to determine if your heart and thinking need to be rerouted to mirror a more positive attitude. Knowledge and skills are the starting point to finding your ambitions, but how you control your thoughts and react to experiences will determine the direction your vision will take.

Once you are inspired, nothing can stand in your way in pursuing your goals. Success will not be measured by how well you compare to others, but how your accomplishments compare to your abilities. [3] "You can change what you are and where you go by what you put in your mind. "Remember that the human brain is similar to the computer-garbage in, garbage out. [4] Feed your mind with healthy positive resources. Take time to meditate and contemplate the direction of your actions and image as you perform your steps toward the destination. [5] "Remember the little world laughs, but the big world will cheer you on to success." [6]

One of my favorite teachers inspired me to write this book. Having been humbled by my inspirations throughout life, I have often taken the time to analyze the different forms of motivation that have occurred in each phase of my life. In childhood, my parents were influential in helping me set my course of action. Now my children are stimulations for me, and encourage me to return the animation for them. In my professional work, inspiration has pulsated from colleagues and students who made positive affirmations about my dreams. Probably the most influential impulses for my ambitions come on a daily basis from students that are still moving toward a "star" or "planet" that might seem too far to reach to the ordinary man, but is a realistic destination to these visionaries. Each has amazing youthful experiences and potential. I see a need to feed inspiration with hope and positive reinforcement that the best is yet to be. I enjoy sitting with each on a one-on-one basis and hearing stories about journeys taken to reach the present situation. The struggles that have been endured which may be as academic as to complete courses to obtain college degrees, or as life threatening as leaving the comforts of home to enter a strange new country. All humans have struggles, but to continue to keep going and striving in the face of adversity displays strength and dedication. The ideal time to listen and evaluate yourself is when you are feeling sky high with success. The endorphins will make your mind a sponge for ideas. [7] The powerful lift that is needed to move you toward your goal is found in a "winning attitude." All the abilities and knowledge will not change your self-image, but exhibiting a "winning attitude" will propel you down the course of your dreams. [8]

I remember being told "When the going gets tough, to tie a knot in the end of the rope and continue your climb." Lean into your support network and hold true to your values. The source of inspiration may be present, but we must allow ourselves to see it by believing and exhibiting a positive attitude. Never give up hope or feel abandoned, because life has not abandoned you. You are worthy. You are a work in progress. You are the crème-de-la-crème. I encourage you to seek success and to discover your inspiration in your experiences from the past and in the present. I find my greatest inspiration comes from helping others get what they want. I hope to develop the desire to identify and guide my own children in seeking inspiration and motivation to accomplish their dreams, because, **Life is an inspiration.**

References:

1. Ziglar, Zig. "How to Be a Winner," CD A Nightingale-Conant Production, 2002. Simon and Schuster Audio.
2. Ibid.
3. Ziglar, op.cit.
4. Ziglar, op.cit.
5. Ziglar, op.cit.
6. Ziglar, op.cit.
7. Ziglar, op.cit.
8. Ziglar, op.cit.

CHAPTER 9
The Attributes of Control

Patience is defined by Webster as "the capacity of calm endurance and tolerant understanding." [1] Parents exhibit patience when they allow their children to learn to walk no matter how many times the children fall. The construction of traditional jigsaw puzzles or the solving for "x" in algebraic equations have a commonality in that the content area is provided, but requires patience to obtain the results. I obtained clarity and understanding of the concept of patience through writing about incidents where patience occurred in my life which leads to a greater level of understanding. Remaining patient means not to become annoyed, but what are the benefits in doing so? Is the use of patience an act of attaining victory through the process of acceptance and gratefulness? Some of the greatest learning moments occur when impatience creates a nonproductive situation. To exhibit patience is an exercise and practice of courage.

The most trying periods of our lives often require us to be the most courageous. Reflecting on difficult times and evaluating the emotional levels of these periods, provides examples of patience through courage or impatience on the brink of a storm. In the reflection are times of fear, anger, belittlement, and distrust. Patience allows the struggle to be resolved by finding and exercising courage to withstand the storm of life. If patience prevailed then the most beautiful moments in life happened. These pivotal moments were incidents that defined character, self-discipline, and self-respect. From these positive developments, the human can find a greater source of response to the next storm in life.

Courage and patience often appear simultaneously. Patience requires finding the inner strength to control anxiety and nervousness. The strength of patience creates an energy that converts negative vibes into positive energy. Patience is an element of allowing one to slow down and see the beauty in the moment itself. "Stop and smell the roses." Patience enables the viewing of small, intricate details that make up the big picture. Consider the jigsaw puzzle; the individual who works on this task has a strategy for completing the picture. The method may be find the corner pieces or place the colors together that match. The process is designated by the person because he sees it as making the work easier. A novice might even dump the entire puzzle on the floor and plan to complete the 1000 piece project in one afternoon, resulting in feeling overwhelmed and ultimately not completing the task in the scheduled time frame. On the other hand a practiced puzzler will place the construction in a place that is free to be used until the task is complete. The puzzle will be in a location that allows freedom from movement or dismantlement until the task is completed. Once the locale is determined, the strategy for construction begins. First, the corner pieces are put in place. Then the process of analyzing and matching the pieces by color or shape is begun. A big mess on a carpeted bedroom floor can be conquered on a card table. The discovery of corners and colors breaks the task into a manageable process, the mess of the whole got less and less. Each piece of the puzzle contributed to a part of a greater display, but patience was required to wait for the big picture. This simple concept applies to other situations. No matter how monstrous life seems to be, define the location for attack; determine the best strategy for accomplishing goals. An example might be accomplishing four life changing goals or reading four chapters of a textbook. The first step is to take courage to believe in self-worth. Then through a process of accepting the situation as to locale and strategy for completing the task, a vision of victory and completion can be seen with the true beauty of the bigger picture. The task is broken into manageable parts. The time frame for completion is established with benchmarks for change in direction or clarity of process. Procedures are set in motion for completing small tasks which ultimately lead to the destination. Learning occurs as the small tasks are completed and movement toward the ultimate end is envisioned. Practicing patience is the key to a victorious success and the reflection leads to pride in the effort.

There is something beautiful about being patient; a level of contentment is realized. Patience allows the expression of thought and courage to build for other stressful times in life. Perhaps the real problem is that patience is often offered as a verbal command, but the process is not taught. Along with the process, the rewards of dreams met and the benefits for future accomplishments must be emphasized. One of the most stressful situations I have encountered was standing on a train platform waiting for a train which was late. I stood on one foot and then the other for some reason thinking this would make the old clock that hung above the platform turn back in time. Two minutes passed and I began to think of an excuse or reason for being late to my meeting. Rather than waste my energy and thoughts on changing something out of my control, I would have been better off considering and practicing mind over matter. I could have controlled my thoughts. I could have directed my thinking to a more positive result. I needed to stop complaining about the delay, I should have envisioned myself where I needed to be. I could have worked on a mental performance of my presentation. Just by imagining what I would say and do, I could improve my dissertation. I also should give thanks that I am where I am. I know it sounds strange to be humble and grateful for an opportunity to mentally focus, but the stress level found by redirecting my thoughts will pay off in my future. All aspects of a stressful situation from finances, the physical stamina to walk through a storm, the ability to stand and wait for the right time, and the ability to see and hear myself are necessary attributes for maturity and success. I am thankful for patience and realize that redirecting my thoughts removes the targets of my negativity.

In conclusion, the virtue of patience is to endure what befalls the individual. Patience is a mere courageous act that requires one to practice mind over matter for a realization of a new angle of perception. Practicing patience builds a repertory of courage and strength. To achieve patience puts one in control and thus obtains a more powerful position. Practicing patience leads to the ability to stop feeling desperate and helpless. It is a positive attribution with qualities that build to a position of control and humbleness. Through time and patience, the inner self begins to see the global view with details of great beauty in the landscape. The worthwhile people and tasks of life require patience and fortitude. To strengthen my endurance for tasks ahead that seem insurmountable, I must determine "what bridges to cross and what bridges to burn." I must analyze the situation as to the locale and strategies, and break the tasks into meaningful units of progress toward the conclusion.

References:

1. The American Heritage Dictionary of the English Language, William Morris, ed. Dallas: Houghton-Mifflin, Company, 1975.

CHAPTER10
The Publication of Intent

The function of sharing feelings, thoughts, and ideas with others with the desire to have them understand and validate the process is a basic need of human beings called communication. Through the dialogue of communication, societies have expressed and recorded events, history, and education. Native Americans sent smoke signals. During World War II, the American forces used Navaho speakers to converse in their native language so the Axis Powers could not decipher the code. Modern text messages use shortened forms of phrases to permit messages to be more succinct. To be effective, communication is a dialogue rather than a monologue. The communication of a message needs a sender to relay meaningful context, through a pathway that permits the receiver to obtain the information and if possible, respond to the message. [1]

The elements of communication are the same for any form of communication. The first component is the sender, the one who begins the conversation. The sender's message reflects his "culture, perceptions, skills, knowledge, attitudes, and experiences." [2] The sender must think through the message, determine the symbols or method to best convey the information, and prepare the presentation. [3] The sender is the one who starts the process as the speaker, the writer, the artist, the telegraph operator, the computer programmer, the videographer, the text writer, etc. [4]

The information that is shared between the sender and receiver is the second component. To avoid miscommunication or misunderstanding, internal barriers must be considered. The most common internal barriers are negativity, distrust, fear, poor listening/reading skills, past experiences, hatred, stress, boredom, and exhaustion. The encoder must reflect on these elements and develop the passage to prevent misunderstanding. Along the same lines, external barriers come into the process. The senders or receivers may not have control of these outside factors which are related to the environment. External barriers may be environment, use of technical language that does not easily convey meaning, time of day, poor connection for transmittal, distractions, noise level, incorrect address, incorrect IP address, busy terminals, and even sunspots. [5]

A channel or method of exchanging the message, between sender and receiver is the third element in communication. Visual channels, written, oral, digital, electronic, sound, a letter carrier, telecasts are just a few of the conveyances used to send and receive messages. Businesses use e-mail, memos, reports, letters, phones, and videos to relay data. Oral methods are best if the message is urgent, personal, or necessitates immediate feedback. When a technical or legal message is sent, written methods allow for documentation. Often data is sent both orally and in writing to guarantee the thoroughness of the decoding by the receiver. [6]

The fourth component of communication is the receiver of the message. The decoder may be a listener, reader, or viewer of the information. [7] The receiver's ability to decipher the message is reflected by his "culture, perceptions, skills, knowledge, attitudes, and experiences." The receiver is also affected by the external and internal barriers of the channel for transmittal. [8] Even when the individual is alone taking notes or writing grocery lists dialogue occurs because the sender is the receiver. The message can be unclear because the sender did not relate all the details, but communication occurs. Case in point, I often get to the grocery store and cannot decipher my handwriting for the items I have on my list. The same external and internal barriers may occur even in self-addressed communication. [9]

The last variable of communication is feedback. Whenever the receiver reacts or responses to the message in a written or oral form, the sender can assume that the information has completed its path. If no response is given, this too may be considered feedback if the message followed its course. The sender can evaluate the feedback to determine the level of success of the information the decoder received. [10]

For communication to be successful and effective, the encoder and decoder must learn to "listen." This requires more than deciphering the message and the symbols. A level of evaluating and thinking about the emotions of the information becomes necessary. The expression of opinions, feelings, and ideas are most effective when the parties respect each other and try to be non-judgmental. Along with the listening to the written and oral, verbal format, the listener needs to interpret the non-verbal clues. Non-verbal signals may be "body movement, gestures, posture, and vocal tone, lack of body movements, eye contact, breathing and muscle tension." [11] A teacher talking to a student about an incident of bad behavior usually watches his eyes and posture. If the student's eyes go to his left during the discussion, the student is probably stating falsehoods. If the student stands with his arms crossed, the listener is not receptive to the message. The non-verbal responses of the teacher can provide positive benchmarks that aid the student's communication to be more reliable. The encoders/decoder's stress level changes the deciphering of verbal and non-verbal clues. The level of stress interrupts creativity, muddles clear thinking, and creates inappropriate responses. Stress can lead to misinterpretations and a failure to compromise. The encoder/decoder must be aware of his emotional level of awareness and attempt to lower the stress level. [12]

Many individuals ask, "Do we communicate with each other better today than we did 40 years ago? Has communication changed with new developments in processes and instruments? In the majority of cases everybody utilizes communication every day. For many years the most common forms of data exchange were verbal and nonverbal. Since the 1960's, an additional dimension has developed with increased processes and instruments from the digital and telecommunication fields. With the movement to these new forms of communication, less face-to-face contact occurs. [13] Emotions were first expressed in electronic messages with standard punctuation, expressions concluding with exclamation marks to denote level of intensity, and use of upper case letters with or without exclamation marks. The digital world added the use of emoticons to provide a form of expression of emotions, negative and positive. Research has shown that the emoticons seem to increase the negative or positive degree of the message, but do little to change the direction of the charge of the message. [14]

Teachers in language classes have noted a marked drop in the ability of students to communicate in written and oral forms. Psychologists state that relationship problems have increased since feelings, gestures, and body language are not necessarily interpreted correctly through digital messaging. Relationships need to be fostered and included in communication. Be sure to "Say what you mean and mean what you say."

References:

1. "Components of Communication," <u>Your Academic Encyclopedia</u>, Business Communication -Notes Desk. 11 March 2009. Online. Retrieved 29 August 2016. 10:00 AM. http://www.notesdesk.com/notes/business-communications/componenets-of-communication.

2. "Understanding Communication Process with 4 Key Elements," Enki Village.com. Retrieved 29 August 2016. 11:00 AM. http://www.enkivillage.com/communication-process.html
3. Ibid.
4. "Components," op.cit.
5. "Understanding," op.cit.
6. "Components," op.cit.
7. "Components," op.cit.
8. "Understanding," op.cit.
9. "Understanding," op.cit.
10. "Components," op.cit.
11. "Understanding," op.cit.
12. "Understanding," op.cit.
13. "What is Communication?" Psychology Today. Online. Retrieved 31 August 2016. 2:00 PM. A video and lesson format. http:// study.com/academy/lesson/what-is-communication-definition-importance.html
14. Ip, Amy. "The Impact of Emoticons on Affect Interpretation in Instant Messaging." Carnegie Melton University: School of Design. Online. Retrieved 3 September 2016, 10:30 AM http://amysmile.com/doc.emotiocon-paper.pdf.

CHAPTER 11

The Manifestation of Honesty

Webster's dictionary defines integrity as "a rigid adherence to a code of behavior, the state of being whole, unimpaired; soundness." [1] Integrity is doing the right thing when no one is looking. Today's world is filled with a need for quick-fixes. Integrity is the character trait that allows the individual to meet challenges that cannot be resolved quickly. [2]

Many times perception is considered to be reality. Perception, sometimes built on shallow acknowledgements, is the focus on the qualities/attributes exhibited and impressions reflected. Integrity is the virtue that is inside. An integrious person always seeks to do the next "right" thing. He may make mistakes, but his inner self-worth can face the error, because he was motivated to make a choice for the good of all. The person with integrity takes responsibility for his own actions. He does not seek someone else to blame or to be identified as a victim. [3]

Anthony Robinson identified ten qualities of a person of integrity:

1. "What you see is what you get. Outer and inner are connected, parts of one whole.
2. A person who has basic integrity honors commitments and keeps promises. If they say they will be there, they are. If they promise to do something, they do it.
3. A person with integrity is truthful. You can trust what they tell you.
4. Consistency. Someone who has integrity isn't your new best friend one week and then next week doesn't seem to know you.
5. Integrity doesn't mean that a person never makes mistakes. But a person with integrity accepts responsibility for his or her own mistakes or failures and does what's in his or her power to put things right.

6. Related to No. 5, people with integrity are slow to blame others for their problems or frustrations. They aren't whiners.
7. People of integrity care about the work, the mission, or the product and about a job well done, and not just about what they personally will get out of it in terms of money, recognition or advancement.
8. While receptive to learning and change, people of integrity are skeptical of simple answers to complex problems, and not inclined toward fads or buzzwords.
9. A person of integrity minds his own business. I don't mean isolation. I mean paying attention to your own responsibilities and work rather than freely inserting yourself into the responsibilities of another.
10. People with integrity know that they aren't perfect and that sometimes in this life it's not possible to avoid disappointing or hurting others. Because of this they are able to forgive and they recognize their own need for forgiveness." [4]

Brian Tracy feels that integrity is the most important quality that a human can possess, since it is the value that "guarantees" all other values. [5]

Tracy notes that character is founded in integrity. An individual works on his character by constantly monitoring his activities and circumstances to exhibit complete honesty. To be honest with others, one must first be honest with self. The person with integrity lives a life based on following his highest values and virtues. One who leads a life with integrity constantly is raising personal thresholds by demanding worthy standards based on honesty. He examines the routine, mundane activities of day-to-day life to assure himself that he is behaving and responding in a manner which reflects self-honesty and integrity. No matter how menial the task, only his best is good enough. Everything the honorable person says, does, and thinks is a statement of his "real" inner self. Starting earlier, working harder, staying later, concentrating on details, and striving to complete every task successfully, displays the art of integrity to others. [6]

Personality is based on a belief system; it can change as needed to fit the occasion or solution. Character is based on a value system. Character is rooted more deeply in the person. Character traits like integrity, tenacity, perseverance, courage, and wisdom develop from associations with people and experiences of life. Character traits represent the true self. Behaviors, values and virtues define the character of a person to himself and the world. [7]

A person who adheres to a life that reflects values of honesty reveals his inner most character. Customers are more willing to do business with a clerk who has integrity than one who is lacking in honesty. Ralph Waldo Emerson stated that you must "Guard you integrity as a sacred thing." (5) Integrity is the number one quality of leadership. One who keeps his word builds trust based on integrity. Constancy, consistency, and confidence echo the value of integrity in a leader.

Reputation, how one is known to others, is an asset in corporations and individuals. One builds a virtuous reputation by keeping promises, fulfilling commitments, and following high standards based on values. To develop integrity, a person should examine role models in the present and history whose character provided them the ability to effectively change the world through thoughts and actions. (9)

Knowledge of the psychology of human behavior allows one to formulate his approach to integrity by acting in a manner consistent with his feelings. The psychology theory of Law of Reversibility, states that "if one acts as if one had a particular feeling, the action will generate the feeling consistent with the behavior." The recovering addict is told to "fake it until you make it." Actions become reality and personality becomes consistent with desires. (10)

Integrity means listening to that inner voice as to what is the right thing to do in a situation. This action leads to a sense of peace and satisfaction which are steps toward success and achievement. Relationships must be built on truth and honesty. One should never do anything or say anything that is contrary to his value system. This also extends to associating with someone whose behavior is incongruent with one's values. A person of integrity cannot stay in a difficult relationship due to stress and negativity. (11)

Another area of concern that demands integrity is finances, money. A person with integrity is cautious with money. Credit ratings, payment of bills, financial commitments, and studious care of money of others reflect integrity. (5) Along this same line, one must be committed to doing what is promised, fulfilling commitments to the best of one's ability, and building trust in circumstances. Every single act of integrity will make character stronger. With the growth of character all parts of life will improve. (12)

Stephen R. Covey, author of <u>The Seven Habits of Highly Effective People</u>, stated that "The degree to which we have developed our independent will in our everyday lives is measured by our personal integrity. Integrity is, fundamentally, the value we place on ourselves. It's our ability to make and keep commitments to ourselves, to 'walk our talk.' It's honor with self, a fundamental part of the Character Ethic, the essence of proactive growth. " [13]

References:

1. The American Heritage Dictionary of the English Language, William Morris, ed. Dallas: Houghton-Mifflin, Company, 1975.
2. Robinson, Anthony B. "Articles of Faith: 10 Qualities you'll Find in a Person of Integrity," Seattle Pl. Com, 27 June 2008. On line. Seattle: Hearst Seattle Media, LLC. http://www.seattlepi.com/local/article/Articles-Of-Faith-10-qualities-you-ll-find-in-a-1277815.php.
3. Ibid.
4. Robinson, op.cit.
5. Tracy, Brian. "Becoming a Person of Integrity,"(1 May 2009)   Brian Tracy International. http://www.personal-development.com/brian-tracy-articles/person-integrity.htm
6. Tracy, op. cit.
7. Akins, Chris. "What is the difference between Values and Beliefs?" 2007. https://www.reference.com/world-view/difference
8. Tracy, op. cit.
9. Tracy, op. cit.
10. Tracy, op. cit.
11. Tracy, op. cit.
12. Tracy, op. cit.
13. Covey, Stephen R. The Seven Habits of Highly Effective People. New York: Simon and Schuster, 1989.

CHAPTER 12
The Perception of the Moment

The modern world of literature and entertainment is filled with books, poems, plays, movies, television shows, artwork, magazines, e-books, music, etc. that have been written or developed by humans who seized the moment of initiative. But I cannot help but wonder how many more literature and entertainment forms might have been created if other crafters had grasp the advantageous circumstances to rise to the occasion and generate unique art forms. It is a sobering thought that a masterpiece, a creation, was lost because someone did not have the courage to act on the opportunity. People write about the opportunities that were present for them, but it is a sobering thought to consider the opportunities that have not been pursued due to caution, or lack of courage. Life is hectic and busy, but it is the busiest of people that achieve their ambitions and dreams because they grab the favorable moments to delve into their passions.

Consider the athletes that competed in the Summer Olympics in Rio, they followed their passions to be the best they could be. They grabbed moments of opportunity to practice their skills and develop their forms. Success did not come to them without investing time and talent in preparing themselves for the ultimate competition. These robust, young talents chased the moments of opportunity so that they could exhibit near perfect abilities in their sports. You too can achieve greatness, but first you must take the initiative to grab at the chances for skills and growth. If there is something that you want to pursue in life such as winning a gold medal, becoming a singer, or finding the dream job, then you must grasp opportunities to train, participate, compete, and seek this ambition. I once thought I wanted to play lacrosse. In middle school lacrosse was offered and I attended practice every day. Lacrosse was not for me, but I seized the trial opportunity to validate my dream and attempt to play. The reason it was not my sport may have been because I was trying to please others when I should have been trying to please myself. School is often the place where you can tryout your dreams and ambitions in a safety net. Other successful ventures I tried were Computer Club and Youth Leadership. These clubs gave me the opportunity to test the waters of membership without fear of failure or disappointment.

A golden opportunity to pursue my dream of writing a book became a reality when I sought the chance to develop this collection of essays. Upon developing a friendship with a colleague I decided to take the initiative and ask Dr. Baethe to co-author this book with me. It required me to overcome the fear that she would decline my request or that I might not be able to fulfill my part due to work and family commitments. As the English proverb says, "Nothing ventured, nothing gained." If I had hesitated or shied away from asking her, I would have missed this opportunity to write. I love writing. I always have and it is what I resort to when life has becomes overwhelming.

As a mother of two small children, I did not know if between work and family I would have time to pursue my lifelong dream of a doctorate degree. My children are a priority in my life, and I feared that I would neglect them if I took the time to follow my dream. Opportunities arose to discuss this fear and analyze solutions so that I now am undertaking this endeavor. Although the next four years may be long and difficult, I know that if I take one day at a time and allow people to support and assist me, I can do this. I will let life happen but stay focused toward my long-range goals. I shudder to think if I had let my fear of "too much" interrupt seeking my goals. I must remember not to let fear direct my life. Good planning, supportive people, and a positive attitude will create a way for everything to work out. I am lucky enough to have rationalized my situation and realized that in the present I have the best of opportunities to reach my ultimate destination. I deserve nothing else but the best.

This same concept can work for you. Discover your inspiration, your sources, and your peace, so you can pursue them with a passion. Avoid being distracted by noise and chaos. Think through the process, develop an inner peace, and allow yourself to believe in your ambitions. Write and develop your plan of action. Pamper yourself with affirmations that reinforce your belief that you can do it. Opportunities are all around you and are accessible if you seize the moment. Be sure that you are not the only thing preventing you from taking advantage of these opportunities. Do not compare the work of others to yours. Every individual comes to the experience with a different background, training, and/or lifestyle. You only have to compete with yourself.

You must strive to make yourself the best that you can be. The fact is that you are unique and have a purpose in this world. It is your responsibility to determine the best way to utilize your talents and abilities to reveal that purpose in life. I encourage you to seek out those chances that will contribute towards creating a more complete you. I challenge you to take the risks involved with accepting the opportunities that lay before you. Permit your mind and body to grow through practice, education, relationships, and experiences to meet life head-on. Utilize the attributes of the people and organizations around you. Apply principles and standards that develop and increase your self-worth and self-esteem. You are a student of this universe and the opportunity to learn is ever present and available. Do not let the fear of anything prevent you from becoming the best that you can be. Follow your dreams and you will be able to be the unique individual you were destined to be.

From the translation of The Rubaiyat of Omar Khayyam, the famous poet states:

"The Moving Finger writes; and, having writ,
Moves on: nor all thy Piety nor Wit
Shall lure it back to cancel half a Line,
Nor all thy Tears wash out a Word of it." [1]

It is your responsibility to make your life have purpose. Once you determine your direction and intent, the process is in motion and will lead you to your dream. I encourage you to write, draw, or do whatever it is that is the pursuit of your passion. Your creation may be the catalyst that causes someone else to attempt to grasp his dream. Your work of art will provide material for thought and growth. Through reading or viewing your creation, others may jump into the pool and try to swim the long course. Don't miss out on the opportunities that lay before you because you didn't take the first step. Stiffen your stance, raise you head high, and be courageous enough to create. Success comes with overcoming the fear of failure and disappointment.

YOU CAN DO IT!

References:

1. Khayyam, Omar. The Rubaiyat of Omar Khayyam, Trans. Edward Fitzgerald. 1859. Print

Section 3 Investments to Reinforce

17. The Component of Excitement -- Passion

18. The Fulfillment of Progress -- Achievement

CHAPTER 13
The Uniqueness of Personality

Character is not easily changed. It reflects the individual's value system, and is often hidden in the depths of his soul. Personality is more variable. It changes based on the circumstances that are surrounding the situation. Personality is a complex attribute that is totally unique to the individual, and only that person can understand what makes him tick. Personality profiling just helps one to gain understanding for the purpose of working out how natural behavior and personal tendencies influence everything that occurs in an individual's life. [1]

Character takes much effort to change and is usually after challenging situations. To determine character traits of kindness, integrity, virtue, etc., the best method is through communicating and evaluating the comments of others that associate with the individual. Personality is often identified in a first impression, but changes based on the situation, the people in attendance, and motivational factors. [2]

To gain information about individuals who are successful, one must question how they act or behave. Analyze personal traits as to the level of assistance these traits contribute to the person's success. The person doing the profiling must compare these traits and the personalities to himself. He must identify the aspects of his personality that will positively or negatively affect the accomplishment of his goals. [3]

Some individuals possess personality traits more in tune with success and achievement than others, but it doesn't mean that everyone else is doomed to failure. Awareness of personality traits that help with achievement on the road to success may become personal characteristics utilized in an advantageous manner to achieve desired results. Along the same lines of thought, the individual must use the skill of discretion to avoid those characteristics that tend to restrain or prevent movement toward the pinnacle of advancement, or at least consider refurbishing them to become "positive drivers." [4]

Personality profiling can help the individual understand himself. Three important personality factors that appear in success theories that define personality and thus help the individual to understand themselves in the trek to accomplishing personal goal setting are:

1. Behavior preferences – Individuals are unique and act differently to unlike situations and things. These natural demeanors affect their perception of success and failure. Dr. William Marston listed four basic behavioral personality types in his DISC theory: D for Dominant, I for Influencer, S for Steady, and C for Compliant. This theory was revised by Dr. Gary Couture into bird names: Dove, Owl, Peacock, and Eagle. Each personality type indicates how individuals interact with other people, live daily lives, are motivated by "personal drivers," and how success is accomplished. One often relates better to people with similar behavior profiles, and finds other profiles to be disturbing or intimidating. Behaviors impact progress through life. [5]

2. Intelligence preferences –Individuals tend to prefer and excel at diverse things, which affect the type goals they set. Intelligence preferences identify the individual's interests. This profile evaluates aptitude. The Intelligence (Aptitude) Preference describes interests, and defines the motivations/desires of the individual. One is most contented and successful when learning, developing, and working through events that are satisfying and rewarding to him. Dr. Howard Gardner, psychologist and professor of education at the Graduate School of Education at Harvard University, through researching 'everyday' people developed the theory of nine intelligences. Dr. Gardner asserts that all people possess all intelligences in varying degrees; yet, each person is vested with a "unique intellectual make-up." These intelligences, located in different areas of the brain, either working independently or together, can be nurtured and strengthened, or ignored and weakened. The nine intelligences which reflect personal preferences, interests, skills, and abilities are: linguistic (verbal), logical (mathematical), musical, spatial (visual), bodily (kinesthetic), interpersonal, intrapersonal, naturalist, and existential. [6]

3. A. Personal motivation – Individuals are motivated by different things, some inherent to personality and some driven by life situations. David McClelland has identified four natural motivators determined by personality:

(1). Achievement- People who sense excitement in achieving difficult goals. These individuals need to feel success at completing their goals and receive feedback along the way concerning their progress.

(2). Authority - People who need to be in control, are perceived as influential, and must have prestige/status. Their egos are satisfied by the acknowledgement of progress toward completing their goals.

(3). Affiliation – People who are "joiners," who love to interact with others, and need to be liked. The joiners need to complete their goals in a team effort.

(4). People who are a combination of these other three. [7]

3. B. Situational motivation - Abraham Maslow developed the Hierarchy of Needs Motivational Model based on five needs. The classification indicates that the lower needs must be met before the higher ranking ones can be attempted. All the levels must be maintained for life to be in balance. The lower levels, deficiency needs, indicate potential pitfalls that can prevent achieving the higher ranked needs. The hierarchy from lowest to highest is:

(1). Biological and Physiological needs – basic survival needs of food, water, shelter, warmth, sleep, health, and air. (**Deficiency needs**)

(2). Safety needs – security, order, law, limits, stability, protection from elements, etc. (**Deficiency needs**)

(3). Social needs – love, family, affection, relationships, friends, work group, etc. (**Deficiency needs**)

(4). Esteem needs – achievement, independence, status, prestige, responsibility, etc. (**Deficiency needs**)

(5). Self-Actualization needs – personal growth, self-fulfillment, realizing personal potential, seeking knowledge and meaning, etc. (**Growth needs**) [8]

Napoleon Hill in his book, <u>The Law of Success</u>, states that "It is the personalities back of a business which determine the measure of success the business will enjoy." [9] Hill stresses the need to "modify" these personalities to be more pleasant and charming to the customers to make the business prosper. Merchandise that is similar in kind and price can be purchased in many stores, but the most successful store is where those in contact with the customer provide pleasant and helpful assistance. The public responds to the winning attitudes of sales clerks and associates. [10]

Hill relates this business success to success in all other aspects of one's life. He defines success as the "the attainment of Definite Chief Aims without violating the rights of other people." [11] He feels that a pleasing personality and gaining the support of others, makes the attainment of goals an easier tasks. Hill encourages the cultivation of a harmonious demeanor and to learn the skills of associating with others in a manner which prevents "friction or envy." [12]

The art of harmonious negotiation is to help people arrange life's circumstances in a manner that reflects "harmony and poise, free from the destructive effects of disagreement and friction which bring millions of people to misery, want, and failure." [13] To obtain success in life an individual needs power and the personality to convince others to cooperate in a "spirit of harmony." [14] [15]

References:

1. Lickerman, Alex. "Personality vs. Character," Psychology Today. 3 April 2011. Web. Retrieved 28 October 2016 2:00 PM.. www.psychologytoday.com
2. Ibid.
3. Jaiper, Jam. "My Life Planning Workbook," 2007. Web. Retrieved 28 October 2016 3:00 P.M. www.achieve-goal-setting-success.com.
4. Jaiper, op.cit.
5. Jaiper, op.cit.
6. Jaiper, op.cit.
7. Jaiper, op.cit.
8. Jaiper, op.cit.
9. Hill, Napoleon. The Law of Success: The Master Wealth-Builder's Complete and Original Lesson Plan for Achieving Your Dreams, Penguin Publishing Group, 2008. (Originally published as 15 pamphlets, 1925, and then as an eight-book series, 1928.)
10. Hill, Law of Success op.cit.
11. Hill, Law of Success op.cit.
12. Hill, Law of Success op.cit.
13. Hill, Law of Success op.cit.
14. Hill, Law of Success op.cit.
15. Ziglar, Zig. "How to Be a Winner," CD A Nightingale-Conant Production, 2002. Simon and Schuster Audio Tape.

CHAPTER 14
The Assurance of Faith

The playwright, Neil Simon, assured individuals of the need to take risks in his quote:

"Don't listen to those who say 'you're taking too big a chance.' If no one ever took risks, Michelangelo would have painted the Sistine floor, and it would surely be rubbed out by today. Most importantly, don't listen when the little voice of fear inside you rears its ugly head and says 'they're all smarter than you out there. They're more talented, they're taller, blonder, prettier, luckier, and they have connections.' I firmly believe that if you follow a path that interests you, not to the exclusion of love, sensitivity, and cooperation with others, but with the strength of conviction that you can move others by your own efforts – and do not make success or failure the criteria by which you live – the chances are you'll be a person worthy of your own respect." [1]

Risk taking should be positively driven and have a definite plan or strategy for implementing the action. Positive risks are taken after much thought and consideration so that a plan is developed. Negative risks are often based on impulse and emotions. An example of positive risks could be returning to school to learn a new skill or trade. Look beyond the scope of the job or career, analysis what is valued and prioritized in the present situation by management. To make this a positive risk, propose new projects along the lines of the valued criteria. Look at the big picture, and expand your horizons. Train for risk taking by grasping small risks, and build up to larger ones so that fear of change is erased by moving in a new direction. Passion will also aid the risk taker in overcoming fear. Analyze others that are performing in the career or job that is being sought. Take notes, read books, search websites, associate with supportive people, practice leadership skills, and write goals that lead to meaningful risk taking. Failure is part of the risk process, but not the end of the game if a lesson is learned through the mistake. The end result of positive risk taking is a payoff upon completion of the tasks. [2]

Ralph Waldo Emerson stated:

"The whole course of things goes to teach us faith. We need only obey.
There is guidance for each of us, and by lowly listening; we shall hear the right word." [3]

Emerson felt that individuals have been born with the inner knowledge of right and wrong. He felt that these concepts are a part of the internal makeup of humans, which he identified as faith. Napoleon Hill had similar theories about overcoming missteps and obstacles along the path of life. He felt that an individual's faith in himself guided him to obtain a certain goal. Faith is described by Napoleon Hill as "a state of mind" which develops voluntarily in the individual who receives training in goal setting, and applies these principles to all phases of his life. "Faith is the 'external elixir' which gives life, power, and action to the impulse of thought." The power of positive self-talk builds the level of faith through diligent affirmations concerning the accuracy, and value of the stated dream, the path to follow, and the steps to take. [4] Hill recognized that positive emotions strengthen thoughts with "vitality, life, and action." Once the subconscious mind is influenced by these emotions, it uses them as pillars for the thought impulses. Positive emotions build positive attitudes; negative emotions build a sense of doom and gloom, fear of misfortune. Practicing control of emotions leads the mind to belief the individual can acquire his dreams and strengthens personal faith in the individual's ability. [5] Hill cautioned about thinking before you speak because other people are influence by your words. He stated, "Think twice before you speak, because your words and influence will plant the seed of either success or failure in the mind of another." [6]

Does this mean that you will never make a mistake, fail in an action, or fall down in a pursuit? On the contrary, as has been viewed in the stories of many successful people, "adversity has a greater or equal benefit" of teaching a lesson for the next time. [7] Hill even went so far as to conclude that all successful people have a difficult start and numerous struggles. Through the throes of crisis, the individual who is able to identify his inner drive and needs will be thrown into a classroom of life toward success. [8] Hill clarified these principles in that defeat is a sign that plans are not sound; therefore, rebuild the plans, and try again. [9] He further cautioned that the most common emotion, fear, leads to thoughts about quitting. Hill felt that listening to this emotion, rather than perceiving how the plan can be reworked is the response of the majority of people who fail. [10] Napoleon Hill further enhanced this principle with the concept that, "Action is the real measure of intelligence." Overcoming fear of a negative behavioral response, use of intelligent self-talk, and listening to positive support of others will motivate the individual who has fallen to get up and move forward. Negative thoughts that indicate the person should wait until a better time destroy self-confidence. Time is not always perfect, but if planning and thought have been used to construct the model, the chances are great that time will not be a deciding factor in the equation for success. [11]

What is the difference between a screw up and a failure? In his audio tapes, "How to be a Winner," Zig Ziglar gives five principles of failure:

1. "Everyone fails from time to time. The real test of a failure is how you pick yourself up and start the journey all over again.
2. Most people make excuses when they fail. Do not resort to these negative responses.
3. People who fail tend to develop poor self-esteem. Poor self-esteem leads to negative attitudes.
4. It is easy to spot negative people. They wear their bad attitudes on their sleeves.
5. You can learn many things by failing. The best thing to learn from failure is not to let it get you down." [12]

Remember that initial passion and desire to follow a dream? Return and relook at that vision, so that imagination and thought can be rekindled. Put aside all doubts and fears. Take the risk to spring toward the completion. [13] As W.E.B. DuBois so aptly said, "The important thing is this . . . to be willing at any moment to give up what you are for what you want to become." A person must give up old habits, memories, behaviors, and thoughts to define his purpose in life. A person's unique self can be stifled by the past. Forge ahead when the path gets rocky; keep your eyes on the end desire. [14]

References:

1. Rooney, David. "Review: 'The Neil Simon Plays: Brighton Beach Memoirs'," Variety, 2009. Online Article. http://variety.com/2009/legit/reviews/the-neil-simon-brighton-beach-memoirs-1200476694.
2. Jones, Gail. "Ten Benefits of Positive Risk-taking," salary.com.
3. Emerson, Ralph Waldo.
4. Hill, Napoleon. Think and Grow Rich. Revised and Edited by Ross Cornwell. San Diego, CA: The Mind Power Institute, Aventine Press, Inc. 2004. Book and Online. (Originally published in 1937.)
5. Hill, Think and Grow Rich, op.cit.
6. Hill, Think and Grow Rich, op.cit.
7. Hill, Think and Grow Rich, op.cit.
8. Hill, Think and Grow Rich, op.cit.
9. Hill, Think and Grow Rich, op.cit.
10. Hill, Think and Grow Rich, op.cit.
11. Hill, Think and Grow Rich, op.cit.
12. Ziglar, Zig. "How to Be a Winner," CD A Nightingale-Conant Production, 2002. Simon and Schuster Audio.
13. Hill, Napoleon. The Law of Success: The Master Wealth-Builder's Complete and Original Lesson Plan for Achieving Your Dreams, Penguin Publishing Group, 2008. Book and Online
(Originally published as 15 pamphlets, 1925, and then as an eight-book series, 1928.)
14. Du Bois, W. E. B. "Passion for Change." Online. http://www.oprah.com/spirit/Be-Ready-at-Any-Moment

CHAPTER 15
The Entrepreneurship of Rapture

What is the key to happiness? Will happiness only be found by solving all the problems of the world, or obtaining all your desires? Dr. Wayne Dyer, noted psychologist, defined happiness as "something that you are and it comes from the way you think." [1] Happiness is not measured by the number of friends on Facebook, or the balance in a checking account. True happiness is based on attitude. [2] A person's attitude is more important than his aptitude. Attitude honors and respects diversity. Perfect performance is not a human feature, but correcting "stinky" thinking is possible by controlling destructive thoughts. Dr. Richard Carlson in his book, Don't Sweat the Small Stuff, provides the idea that contentment is found by paying attention to thoughts and eliminating those that are "self-defeating." [3]

The Roman emperor, Marcus Aurelius, in his book, Meditations, stated that "The happiness of your life depends upon the quality of your thoughts." [4] Troublesome thoughts are perceived as reality when the truth is that the human mind is a sea of swirling thoughts. The individual has created these thoughts and has the power to discern the images of mental vision growing from these ideas as a truly helpful concept or a nightmare. If the thoughts are building into stress, anger, and unhappiness, self-talk halts the flow of absurd apparitions that haunt life. [5] A person can take thoughts less seriously than as reality by acknowledging that the ideas came from circumstances and fly away when a different situation arises. [6]

Marcus Aurelius' analysis of happiness was "Very little is needed to make a happy life; it is all within yourself in your way of thinking." [7] Good moods build optimism and confidence. Bad moods breed pessimism and hopelessness. Happiness can be destroyed during a time of misery if the person attempts to fix what is wrong. Figuring out what is wrong and fixing it during times of perceived doom and gloom often leads to fatal confrontations, destruction of relationships, and blockage of communication [8] Judgment is not at its best during the siege of woe and forlornness. The individual should postpone reacting to situations and issues. If something must be acted upon, he must remember that the appraisal of the situation is clouded with darkness and foreboding, so work cautiously toward resolution. One must also respect the rights of others to have a bad day by distancing himself from the person, and under no circumstances should he offer advice. [9]

The civil rights activist of the 1960's, Martin Luther King, Jr., said, "Those who are not looking for happiness are the most likely to find it, because those who are searching forget that the surest way to be happy is to seek happiness for others." Opinions are as varied as the situations from which they arise. A person's perspective is influenced by his unique life situations and experiences. This diversity in life causes a variegated array of opinions, and a multitude of attitudes toward happiness. The person seeking happiness strives to understand and respects the dissimilar views of others. This empathy and consideration of another's point of view breaks down the defenses of all parties involved so compromise is possible. [10]

Daphne du Maurier, in her novel, Rebecca, stated, "Happiness is not a possession to be prized; it is a quality of thought, a state of mind." When a person is sensing negativity, anger, jealousy, frustration, and gloominess, an alarm should go off that his thinking is destructive and dysfunctional. Reacting to these repugnant cognitions unfold into psychological peril. One must consider the circumstances that created these sources of tension and replace them with more pleasant images. Calm, contented sensations lower stress levels, improve reactions to others, and decrease harmful effects of tension on the human body. [11]

The great comedian, Groucho Marx, stated, "I, not events, have the power to make me happy or unhappy today. I can choose which it shall be. Yesterday is dead, tomorrow hasn't arrived yet. I have just one day, today, and I'm going to be happy in it." Richard Carlson suggested a need to seek beauty in the present. Fear of "could a," "would a," and "should a," or more appropriately described as worrying about the past and fretting about the future, destroys the richness of today. Carlson encouraged one to focus on the today to free the mind of distractions and fear. From the calm attention to the here- and-now, the person promotes a sense of inner balance and peace. [12]

Gordon B. Hinckley, religious leader, stated that, "Generally speaking, the most miserable people I know are those who are obsessed with themselves; the happiest people I know are those who lose themselves in the service of others . . . By and large, I have come to see that If we complain about life, it is because we are thinking only of ourselves." Why are many people reluctant to feel happy? Dr. Richard Carlson in his book, Don't Sweat the Small Stuff at Work, felt that an individual who was "enthusiastic, light-hearted, inspired, relaxed, or happy – especially at work" was perceived by fellow workers or employers as one who did not work hard or was too satisfied with things to work for improvement. Necessary motivation was judged to be lacking and this individual could not survive in a "competitive environment." [13] Carlson stated that these perceptions were false. He believed that happy people "love what they are doing" and thus they were highly motivated to perform better and more efficiently. [14] He also discerned that these people had good listening skills and exhibited "charismatic" aura that allowed them to be great team players. Happiness allowed a person to be creative, empathetic, relaxed, forgiving, motivated, inspired, and driven. The happy person saw answers and solutions to problems. The rapture of having a burst of energy from the cheerfulness permitted one to be "level-headed" and to overcome adversity and setbacks. [15]

The definition of happiness is a personal self-affirmation of the individual. Control of thoughts leads to control of happiness which is powerful. Susan Polis Schutz, poet, felt that "This life is yours. Take the power to choose what you want to do and do it well. Take the power to love what you want in life and love it honestly. Take the power to walk in the forest and be a part of nature. Take the power to control your own life. No one else can do it for you. Take the power to make your life happy." Picture the definition of happiness by placing your right pointer finger on your right temple and your left pointer finger on your left temple. Hypothesis and conclusion is that happiness is between your fingertips.

References:

1. Dyer, Dr. Wayne. Change Your Thoughts – Change Your Life, Hays House, Published on December 1, 2011. Book and DVD
2. Carlson, Richard, PHD. "Keys to Real Happiness," Don't Sweat the Small Stuff. New York: Hyperion Press, 1997. Book
3. Carlson, op.cit.

4. The Roman emperor, Marcus Aurelius, in his book, <u>Meditations</u>, 161- 180 AD. Online article.
5. Carlson, op.cit.
6. Carlson, op.cit.
7. Aurelius, *op. cit.*
8. Carlson, op.cit.
9. Carlson, op.cit.
10. Carlson, op.cit.
11. Carlson, op.cit.
12. Carlson, op.cit.
13. Carlson, Richard, PHD. "Keys to Real Happiness," <u>Don't Sweat the Small Stuff at Work</u>. New York: Hyperion Press, 1998. Book
14. Carlson, <u>Work</u>, op.cit.
15. Carlson, <u>Work</u>, op.cit.

CHAPTER 16
The Reassurance of Ambition

A ccording to Webster, encouragement is the act of inspiring, stimulating or giving help. "Simply showing genuine interest in someone else is a powerful source of encouragement." [1] Some people have the gift to encourage others with words, a smile or even a touch. "Anyone can be an encourager. This gift is not dependent on age, size, capabilities or education." [2] Everyone needs encouragement; while some are encouragers, others are recipients of the encouragement.

When Qunoot asked me to co-author this book, we began to discuss the various topics to include. We both made lists of the topics we felt were important for all ages; encouragement was one of the topics. I have been a recipient of encouragement and believe strongly in the positive benefits; as I have grown and matured through the years, I have found myself being an encourager. I believe that is how we pay forward for all of the good things that we have experienced in life. This chapter will include my real-life experience with encouragement. It focuses on the powerful influence that people have on others. Family, friends, and teachers have daily opportunities to mold lives, reinforcing the belief that words, actions and simple gestures do make a difference.

At my birth, my parents chose to name me Barbara after my Aunt Barbara, a lady who has the 'encouragement' gift. She gives encouragement to everyone she meets, including me, her name sake. She makes me feel as though I can do anything. If we feel special encouragement, we will work to do our best. I have thought about all the people during my life who have encouraged me the most. Most of us have people who have helped us set and accomplish goals. This little book does not have enough pages to acknowledge the countless numbers of individuals who have inspired, stimulated and given me hope over the past years.

Parents are usually our first encounter with encouragement. My parents always encouraged me to try new, more challenging tasks. I still do this. From my earliest remembrance, my Grandmother was a source of encouragement. She thought that I was brilliant even before I could write my name and that I was perfect in spite of all of my faults. She never met a stranger and lived by the Golden Rule, which is something that I have continued.

Mrs. Stewart, my first grade teacher had a unique way of making all of her students feel good about themselves and their abilities. Her encouragement became the foundation upon which my self-confidence was built and has directed my life. It has been the same approach that I have used with all of my students. Another major encourager of mine was Mrs. Pontiff; she was my typing teacher in high school and was also the sophomore class sponsor the year that I was class president. I became acquainted with her not only as a teacher, but also as a person. She treated all of her students the same and made us feel good about ourselves. While I loved my first grade teacher dearly, I would have to say that Mrs. Pontiff was my all-time favorite teacher --and there have been many. Those who have tried to read my handwriting are eternally grateful that she taught me how to type, as penmanship is not my area of strength. She used to put notes in our typewriters at our assigned stations. On Monday after we had our Sophomore Sweetheart Dance, the major event of my presidency, she placed a book of quotes at my station and had underlined one. "Duty makes us do things well, but love makes us do them beautifully." It is amazing what a few words can do to motivate. As educators, we have noted through the years that a little encouragement can make the difference for some students to keep trying and remain in school.

My great-aunt, affectionately known as Auntie, encouraged many people during her 70+ years of teaching and nearly 100 years of life. I am grateful to have been one of them. She never married and maintains that "it is better to live your whole life wanting something you didn't have, than to live your whole life having something you didn't really want in the first place." She always said she was not an old maid, rather a living monument to man's stupidity. Her wonderful sense of humor encouraged everyone she ever met to be positive and to make lemonade when given a lemon. Her life was an inspiration to all who knew her.

My dearest friend, Virginia has been a mentor, friend, confidant and encourager to me since I received my first teaching assignment. In 1971, I discovered myself teaching across the hall from her room. Her love for knowledge was contagious and before long, I had enrolled in graduate school with her. After I got married, she said,

"You will probably never finish your master's degree." She knew that this was all the encouragement I needed to prove her wrong. How proud she was I went on to receive a doctorate degree! Her belief in me has been a constant source of encouragement for me to achieve higher goals than I ever imagined.

My life has been full of individuals who have encouraged me. I realize that not everyone has such a story, which is all the more reason that you need to find those people who will be the encouragers in your life and then, pay it forward, too.

Drew Dudley describes learning from a young woman that years earlier, when passing out lollipops on campus to promote Shinerama, -- which is Students Fighting Cystic Fibrosis charitable cause, he had made a brief, but huge impact that changed the course of her life. In his presentation, he defines this as a "lollipop moment," a moment when someone says or does something that makes another person's life better, sometimes without ever fully realizing the impact of that moment. [3] He equates encouragement to leadership. You can hear this entire talk and others by visiting http://www.ted.com/talks/drew_dudley_everyday_leadership

In order to maximize your potential, you must surround yourself with people who bring you joy and avoid those who bring you down. I believe that we can accomplish anything we want in life; we are only limited by the perimeters of our imagination and a desire to overcome obstacles that merely slow us down. We can accomplish and achieve in spite of the difficulties along the way. Having those encouragers in our lives makes it easier; some of us have been surrounded by encouragers since we were born, which is a huge advantage. Those not so fortunate can find encouragers that will make the difference. To paraphrase what Drew Dudley talked about, we may never know the impact we have on a person even if it turns out to be a major source of encouragement that changes a life for the better. It has been said that most people, regardless of age or position, do not care how much a person knows. They want to know how much a person cares. I would encourage each of you to be encouragers as you are touching those whose lives cross your path and seek encouragers in your own lives.

References:

1. Tchividgian, GiGi Graham, A *Search for Serenity*, 1990. Portland, Oregon: Multnomah Press, p. 185.

2. Ibid.
3. Chesney, M.L. Perfect Gifts: Time, Encouragement, and Expertise, Journal of Pediatric Health Care, November-December, 2014, Vol. 28, Issue 6, pp. 467-468. DOI: http://dx.doi.org/10.1016/j.pedhc.2014.08.001

Resource
Dudley, D. (2010, September). Drew Dudley: Everyday leadership [video file]. Retrieved from: http://www.ted.com/talks/drew_dudley_everyday_leadership

CHAPTER 17
The Component of Excitement

Passion can take many forms. Webster defines passion as, "any powerful emotion or appetite such as, love, joy, hatred, anger, or greed . . . the boundless enthusiasm for the object of that emotion or appetite." [1] Passion is the zeal to have an object or participate in one of life's activities that enhances and sparks the person's energy, motivation, and sense of purpose.

In April 2013, Jim McIngvale, better known as Mattress Mack of Gallery Furniture, presented a speech, "Ten Tips for Success," to the scholarship recipients of the American Advertising Federation. In the speech he quoted Confucius, **"find a job you love to do, you'll never have to work a day in your life**." [2] He encouraged the scholars to, "Find your life work; this will be your passion." [3] Jim related a story of an intern in heart surgery at Ben Taub Hospital, Dr. Billy Cohn, who also worked full time at the emergency room. Billy worked a minimum of 150 hours a week. He was doing what he did best, saving lives. Twenty years after Jim's first introduction, he again met Dr. Billy Cohn, then a heart specialist at St. Luke's Hospital, who was called in to save George McIngvale. George, Jim's brother, was suffering from congestive heart failure. Dr. Cohn still was working lengthy hours. One night about two in the morning, Jim was visiting his brother, when Dr. Cohn made his rounds of the ICU unit caring for patients. Jim asked him, "What time do you operate in the morning?" Dr. Cohn answered, "Oh, we operate at about six." Jim said, "Don't you ever get tired?" In a matter of fact way, Dr. Cohn answered, "This is what we do." Billy Cohn thrived on his passion of service, and gained strength plus perseverance from saving the lives of others. [4]

If an individual's passion is the joy of work, work will be reflected in the attitude that defines that person. A teacher friend of mine took retirement after 38 years to

care for her elderly mother. The mother only lived a few months after the friend's retirement, and the friend wanted to return to teaching. The State of Texas at that time
was not encouraging retired teachers to return to the classroom, so my friend began
to seek other forms of teaching. She did not feel that she was a whole individual until
she located a teaching job at a private elementary school. She had always worked as
a teacher and defined herself as a person who facilitated others to obtain knowledge
and skills. My friend had set a goal for teaching that she measured her success based
on her ability to help other people get what they wanted through knowledge and
skills. Her passion was kindled by the opportunity to teach and her life was given
purpose through her work in education.

Lt. Colonel Jay Brewer Associate Director of the Aggie Band noted the passion for
music of Colonel Joe Tom Haney, Director Emeritus of the Fighting Aggie Band. In a
eulogy of March 2016, Brewer related stories of Haney's search throughout his life to
instill a love of music in his students. Brewer noted that the World War II vet had always had the desire to share his fervor for helping others to reach success in the music
field. [5]

Prior to coming to Texas A & M in 1972, Colonel Haney had directed numerous high school bands across Texas. Through his leadership of young band members, Haney encouraged and demanded practice and discipline of his students.
Hours were spent by Colonel Haney guiding, teaching, and modeling fortitude and
strength, which were reflected in the numerous awards, honors, and invitations to
perform that were bestowed on these high school band members. Haney rewrote
music to simplify the strands for the novice musicians, but in no way did the rewrites
destroy the beauty of the music. All of his students did not become great musicians,
but the majority of them credit his band classes "for giving them a life shaping influence, for developing self-discipline, for building personal and group responsibility,
for instilling the desire to strive for excellence, for cultivating the need to care for
others, and for bestowing an enduring love of music." [6] His example gave instruc-
tion in the work ethic, in how to have a successful family and career, and in how
self-respect plus a good attitude are personal attributes. Haney shared through
encouragement and praise his love of music and his fellowman. This ardor was expressed in his comments such as, "only your best is good enough," "let's try that one
more time, so all will get it right," or "remember if you do it right the first time, you
will not have to find the time to do it over." [7] Haney developed the intricate maneu-
vers and precisions displayed at half times by military bands. This enthusiasm for

music and people was reinforced through Haney's music composition skills. Haney was recognized and honored by his peers. Prior to coming to A&M, Haney was credited with writing for the Aggie Band such notable tunes as "Gig 'Em," and the march "Noble Men of Kyle." Colonel Haney put his energy and life into providing others the opportunity to become the best that they could be. [8]

Braden Thompson in his article for Lifestyles, "What it Means to Have Passion," states that passion is an emotion that must be acted upon or it has no worthwhile results. [9] Passion gives a person the strength to continue fighting in difficult times to reach a dream or goal. Passion also requires diligent effort, defying vulnerability, and hard work. It is not always the destinations that are important in the pursuit of passion, rather it is the path to follow to seek the dream. Thompson encourages his readers to try new things to determine their passion, and not give up. He feels that remaining in a comfort zone; rather than looking for a higher level of achievement is a destructive force in the search for passion. [10] The author further states that all the passion in the world is not an emotion until the individual dares push aside obstacles and failures to seek a true fulfillment in the journey through life. Life is not a dress rehearsal. Live every day as if it were your last. [11]

References:

1. The American Heritage Dictionary of the English Language, William Morris, ed. Dallas: Houghton-Mifflin, Company, 1975.
2. "You Tube Video Originally written as a Pivot commercial" Written on January 24, 2014. 53 seconds. Retrieved August 27, 2016. 6:00 AM. https://www.youtube.com/watch?v=nq7dngBNJPU
3. McIngvale, Jim. "You Tube. 28:31. Published July 2, 2013. **Jim "Mattress Mack" McIngvale's Speech to AAF Scholarship Winners – April 2013** Retrieved August 14, 2016. 2:00 PM. https://www.youtube.com/watch?v=evBFXc0ZBvY. (Video) **https://www.facebook.com/mattressmack/posts/635747513111431 (Transcript)**
4. McIngvale, op.cit.
5. Brewer, Jay. "A Service of Witness for the life of Joe Tom Haney," Eulogy presented on March 14, 2016, Bryan, Texas.
6. Ibid
7. Ibid.
8. The Bryan Eagle, "Obituary Section," "Haney, Joe." 14 March 2016.

9. Thompson, Braden. "What it Means to Have Passion." <u>Lifestyle</u>. Online Article. http://www.lifehack.org/articles/lifestyle/what-it- means-to-have-passion.

10. Ibid.

11. Ibid.

CHAPTER 18
The Fulfillment of Progress

"What the mind can conceive and believe, the mind can achieve." [1] "The act of accomplishing or completing something" is the definition of achievement by Webster. [2] Webster also stressed the important part of the process to be "the act of completing through exertion, skill, practice or perseverance" [3] Napoleon Hill believed that the steps to reach the culmination are as important as arriving at the final destination.

Napoleon Hill, an American writer and public speaker, authored the personal-success book, <u>The Law of Success in Sixteen Lessons</u>, based on the theories of success of Andrew Carnegie and Hill's interviews of over 500 successful men and women. Hill discovered and published his formula for success in 1925, and changed it into a training course in 1940. This course, with its principles, is still used today in business and educational circles. [4] One of his most quoted principles concerns the relationship between achievement and desire. Hill felt, "Desire is the starting point of all achievement, not a hope, not a wish, but a keen pulsating desire which transcends everything." [5] The factors that permit an individual to set into motion the process for success are: set a specific definite goal to achieve, determine the exact steps to reach that goal, establish a deadline for completion of the goal, develop and begin immediately to set an action plan in place, prepare a written concise statement of the intended goal and all steps to accomplish this objective, read and affirm these goals as a vision twice daily. [6] The development of this prescription allows dreams to become reality. The small steps along the pathway are opportunities to move toward the end result. The growth of self-esteem and development of personal satisfaction along the route assists the individual to continue his struggle to the top. The desire must be an obsession that abounds past all other ambitions, the view of the end is constantly set at the apex of the climb. The vision of the end plus the personal positive affirmations of progress toward the goal reinforces the persistence of the goal-seeker to continue to strive for the pinnacle. Thus Hill stated that the quality a dreamer must possess to change ambition to reality is "definite knowledge of what one wants, and a burning desire to possess it."[(7)] "The greatest achievement was, at first, and for a time, but a dream." [(8)]

To achieve the individual must know his "other self." Through self-analysis and to look for the goodness inside of his soul, an individual can change self-talk, attitude, and habits to allow potential to emerge. The great ability of Walt Disney would have never been realized by others except that he allowed his imagination to expand his mental horizons. Napoleon Hill states that "men are driven to drink and women to ruin" if they allow disappointment or setbacks to overpower their projected goals and dreams. Hill encouraged individuals in the throes of strong emotional struggles to reach inside themselves to the dreams and "transmute" those emotions into constructive actuality. [(9)] A wish is a dream in the heart, but the true test of obsession is to be ready to acquire that reward. The secret to achieving is to believe in self. Open-minded acceptance that the dream is possible "inspires faith, courage, and belief." [(10)] The effort to demand abundance, prosperity, and success is equivalent to the energy expended in misery and poverty. It takes more facial muscles to frown than it does to smile. [(11)]

Hill revealed the Golden Rule of Achievement, "an individual who seeks success must work harmoniously in co-operation with other individuals or groups of individuals and thus creating value and benefit for them will create sustainable achievement for oneself." [(12)] Booker T. Washington had many reasons not to be successful; two of which were he was born in slavery and had to overcome racial strife. Washington set a model for an entire race through his open mindedness and ability to be tolerant of the opinion of others. Booker T. Washington was a dreamer/teacher who helped others reach their potentials. Hill felt that only by helping others achieve their dreams and goals, could an individual be successful in life. Hill stressed the need for cooperation, teamwork, and congeniality to work toward a successful conclusion. Failure occurs when discourse, jealously, greed, selfishness, and hubris pride become the motivation rather than positive attitude combined with a desire to work in tandem for a common goal. The individual must plant in others the seed that an attitude of faith in self will grow into the reality of achievement. [(13)] Hill envisioned that successful individuals were "cheerleaders" for the clients they led. In the fall of 1970, a wise principal of a small junior high school encouraged his faculty to be "cheerleaders" for their students who might have doubts or fears about being able to achieve success. Through regular "pep talks" this educator instructed his group of teachers. He became a cheerleader for each of them. He modeled the belief that each and every one of those educators was capable of teaching any course or student that passed his way. He always left encouraging notes and messages when a teacher had a difficult task. He spoke only positive comments to the board and other administrators about "his people." He built a family of congeniality so that each teacher felt secure in asking him or a fellow teacher for help. Persistent desire for achieving success and a vision of what the end result would be allowed adults and children to be given knowledge and skills to lead successful lives. [14]

The human mind has the power to "utilize every circumstance, every individual, every physical thing" into a physical counterpart. The physical component represents energy, motivation, self-reliance, integrity, and faith. Napoleon Hill believes that "faith in individuals, combined with desire transmitted through persistent, continuous effort, and trust in the worth of others" provides opportunities for growth and achievement. [15] Napoleon Hill determines that, "If you cannot do great things, do small things in a great way. There are really no small steps, but sub steps that lead to the ultimate goal. Every step must lead toward the vision that has been set in the individual's mind." [16] Hill defines this as "mental chemistry," a "wish to convey a thought that all achievements, no matter what may be its nature, or purpose, must begin with an intense desire for a definite and specific goal." [17]

References:

1. Hill, Napoleon. <u>The Law of Success: The Master Wealth-Builder's Complete and Original Lesson Plan for Achieving Your Dreams,</u> Penguin Publishing Group, 2008. Book and Online (Originally published as 15 pamphlets, 1925, and then as an eight-book series, 1928.)

2. <u>The American Heritage Dictionary of the English Language</u>, William Morris, ed. Dallas: Houghton-Mifflin, Company, 1975.

3. Ibid.

4. Hill, Napoleon. <u>Think and Grow Rich</u>. Revised and Edited by Ross Cornwell. San Diego, CA: The Mind Power Institute, Aventine Press, Inc. 2004. Book and Online. (Originally published in 1937.)

5. Hill, <u>Think and Grow Rich</u>, op.cit.

6. Hill, <u>Law of Success</u>, op.cit.

7. Hill, <u>Law of Success</u>, op.cit.

8. Hill, <u>Think and Grow Rich</u>, op.cit.
9. Hill, <u>Law of Success</u>, op.cit.
10. Hill, <u>Think and Grow Rich</u>, op.cit.
11. Hill, <u>Think and Grow Rich</u>, op.cit.
12. Hill, <u>Law of Success</u>, op.cit.
13. Hill, <u>Law of Success</u>, op.cit.
14. Hill, <u>Law of Success</u>, op.cit.
15. Hill, <u>Think and Grow Rich</u>, op.cit.
16. Hill, <u>Think and Grow Rich</u>, op.cit.
17. Hill, <u>Law of Success</u>, op.cit.

49532525R00050

Made in the USA
San Bernardino, CA
27 May 2017